Church Monastery
Cathedral

Herbert Whone

Church Monastery Cathedral

*A Guide to the Symbolism of the
Christian Tradition*

Drawings by Denys Baker
based on sketches by the author

Compton Russell Element

© Herbert Whone 1977

First published in Great Britain by
Compton Russell Ltd
The Old Brewery, Tisbury, Wiltshire
and printed there by
The Compton Press Ltd

Designed by Humphrey Stone

ISBN 0 85955 031 1

Introduction

It occurred to me some years ago that though there is an increasing interest in ancient monuments, people visiting them do so rather aimlessly. Guide books to our churches, monasteries, and cathedrals, are often available, it is true, but the terms in them are not generally understood. The result is that though there is plenty to see, there is little conscious looking. I found my own children, for instance, constantly asking me the meanings of words and where this or that was to be found in the church. Because of this, and because of my own long-standing fascination with churches and in the subject of symbolism, I undertook to make a glossary of any word that one would be likely to find in a guide book, so that sight-seeing should be more intelligible and more enjoyable for a wide cross-section of people.

As the work took shape I saw that a particular thing had to be taken in its fullest sense. First, there was the simple etymology, the fascination of language – the interest of knowing, for instance, that 'canopy' is derived from the shape of a gnat's eye. Then there was the symbolism of a given thing, often inherent in its name, as with the word 'nave', for instance, where the essential meaning is from Latin *navis*, indicating the ship or ark which is a vehicle for the spirit riding upon the waters of life. There were too the historical facts about a thing, interesting in their own right, simply because the existence of a thing now is determined by its roots in the past. And lastly there were purely architectural words needing explanation, and here I realised that it would be pointless to make an academically exhaustive research, since there are many excellent reference books in that field. The aim has been throughout to stimulate interest in the religious buildings and their contents, which are being held by ordinary people in increasing veneration, with special reference to familiar words which may have been too long taken for granted.

I have a special interest in symbolism, as the reader will discern, for, especially in dealing with such a fundamental subject as religion, the inner is inevitably seen to take on an outer form. The external temple, certainly, is the church, but the real temple is man's own inner temporal being. And there is a deep relationship between the two. We see, for instance, that oil and wax (see under 'Christ' and 'candle' respectively) are constantly used in the church for providing light, and that the property of both is to make for smooth inter-action of parts, whether it be a human being or a machine. Oil is used as a lubricant externally and internally and is clearly a harmonising agent. But everything exists on three planes, an obvious physical one, a psychological one, and an unconditioned spiritual one. Oil is an actual physical embodiment of something from the middle one of those planes, something we call love, which on the highest plane, as Love, is normally beyond our comprehension. This is especially significant since Christ's central message is one of love, and when a man is truly able to love his neighbour, he has finished his work on earth. The point to realise is that such a symbol does not arbitrarily find its way into the church. Oil and wax give the light of true understanding which is from the heart and they are not abstractions merely *representing* love – they have assumed the property of love. In the same way trees and plants have assumed in their external form, inner qualities, and in fact all things are merely signatures of inner properties. It has to be remembered too that the working of correspondences lies in the principle of the microcosm and the macrocosm (the small world and the great world) – that all in the universe is within man, giving a relationship between him and nature on all levels. Thus a symbol already lives in him, and for a man to know one, he has first to recognise it as a part of himself.

Again we have in the symbol of the cross a simple crossing of two lines, an archetypal image of all duality – two forces at variance. Man's cross is his dual nature. On the physical level the prison of the body is at variance with the freedom of the spirit; on the psychological level, these opposing pulls give rise to great suffering and conflict (a cross state), and on the highest conceivable level there is the fundamental duality in Absolute power, which once the act of creation has been initiated, has divided itself into *creator* and *created*. Is there any wonder that the church building came to embody this meaning, for it cuts through all levels – it is the root of life. It can be seen therefore, that a symbol may be taken on many different levels – it deals indirectly with truth as with the parables in the New Testament, and I make no claim to cover all possibilities of interpretation, merely to provide what I consider to be an essential key. I am indebted to the long and varied tradition of the inner teachings, to men who throughout the ages have seen the outer as a mere cloak on the inner, and by whose help I have been enabled to arrive at my own structure of understanding.

One thing which recurs constantly in this symbolism is a strange dialectic, for opposites live within each other. Everywhere, visible evil can be seen to contain the seeds of good and conversely good has only grown out of what has been considered evil. If the reader turns to the heading 'church' he will see that the ring or circle, though essentially a symbol of eternity is also a symbol of limitation. If he turns to the heading 'cross' he will see that the transfixing is only one aspect, the negative aspect of it, and the freedom lies in that very point, the still point of the cross that most resembles death. If he turns to the heading 'five wounds', he will find that this fifth point is the key to man's evolution – that though there is a devilish aspect in it, there is also the potentially developed man *in control* of his five senses. The reader will find such paradoxes everywhere, as again in the word Lucifer which though being the name of the Prince of Darkness also means 'bringer of light'. This sort of paradox extends equally to Satan, Sun and Moon, Alpha and Omega, and elsewhere. Man's purpose on earth, given his condensed physical body and his hard egotism, is to re-find his will, to relate the spirit to the body so that he is no longer disturbed by such apparent dualities.

The return journey is the 'work'. The enemy is always the external form; man's inner awareness tends to seep outwards to what his eyes see so that he enumerates facts about a thing rather than seeking to understand what it really *is*. As soon as an image is erected, representing some aspect of Divinity, the danger is that the image rather than the power itself is worshipped. Man is so fascinated by the outer form that Christ's simple message of inner change and love was subject to the same fate. When it became dogmatised, Church-men were so spell-bound by words and by their own infallibility that they were prepared to kill in defence of them. What has this to do with religion? Nevertheless, despite this, the church building contains the secrets of spiritual truths, and the medieval period was the apogee of their perfect embodiment, just as the violin reached its perfected form in the 17th century. Function and form in both cases became one, and all flowered from a germ of inner meaning. The message of the cross is fundamentally one of pain leading to love and true knowledge: the movement is from water to spirit, from foot to head in the church. It is a pity that so much meaning has been lost sight of, that now there is so much arbitrariness in the form of Non-conformist churches and their contents. The Reformation wiped away excesses in iconography and worship of idols in order to recover the inner man, but it also wiped away a tradition of symbolism which is hard to recollect when we step into our ancient monuments. It is this I have attempted to recover in this glossary.

I also believe that there is a limit to the rational philologist's explanations of word origins: there are basic roots it is true, and these are stated first throughout the book, but there is also an intelligent force giving away secrets so to speak, through words, and though they may differ in time and place, the result is that many words related by sound or spelling or anagram, are above man's reason – they come like the elements of a magical musical performance, undefinably and from a different level. Such a state holds, I believe, in such words as 'Son', 'altar', 'Devil', 'bell', 'tree' and so on. For the etymological findings however, I am indebted largely to H. C. Wyld's *Universal Dictionary of the English Language*.

For architectural and historical data I would like to acknowledge my indebtedness to various sources, especially *Glossary of Architecture*, J. H. Parker, *History of Architecture*, Bannister Fletcher, *English Architecture,* T. D. Atkinson, *Monumental History of the British Church*, J. Romilly Allen, *English Church Craftsmanship*, Fred Crossley, and *English Monasteries*, Samuel Fox. I have also referred to *Sacred and Legendary Art*, Jameson, *Symbolism in Christian Art*, F. E. Hulme, and *Brewer's Dictionary of Phrase and Fable*. As I wrote the book, I found myself tending to be generous in the scope of the words considered, so that some may not appear to have much to do with either the outside or the inside of the visible church, nor even a museum attached to it. Such are 'sacrament' and 'ascension'. Where this occurs I felt that inclusion would add to the general understanding of the Church and the church building. Ideally perhaps, the whole would have been better written free from the restriction of the form of a glossary, but I decided finally that this was the only satisfactory way of presenting the material. My aim, as I have said, has been to stimulate interest on many levels, and in different people, and I can not hope to have the approval of all. But if the improvement in the once half-hearted wanderings of my own family, and the renewed interest of some of my friends are anything to go by, my aim will have been fulfilled.

Harrogate, 1976

HERBERT WHONE

Note on Symbolism

The following entries deal with symbolism, and the reader may benefit from reading them separately so as to establish a core of inner meaning:

Adam and Eve	Evangelist	Organ
Alpha and Omega	Fish	Pall
Altar	Five wounds	Passion
Amen	Font	Pillar
Apocalypse	Freemason	Right and Left
Ascension	Garden of Eden	Rood
Ass	Glory	Rose
Baptistery	Halo	Rose-window
Bell	Icon	Sacrament
Blessing	Jesse tree	Satan
Book	Key	Sacrarium
Candle	Lamb	Serpent
Chalice	Last Judgement	Spire
Christ	Last Supper	Stoup
Church	Lectern	Sun and Moon
Crucifixion	Lily	Swan
Cock	Lucifer	Swastika
Colour	Lion	Temple
Column	Magi	Tomb
Cross	Man	Transept
Crozier	Mandorla	Trinity
Devil	Mason	Trumpet
Disciple	Mass	Tympanum
Doom	Maze	Unicorn
Dove	Monogram	West end
Dragon	Nativity	Wine
Eagle	Nave	Virgin Mary
East end	Noah	Yew

The church as a journey from West to East

A

ABACUS

Latin, from Greek *abakos*, originally a square board covered with sand upon which figures could be traced. Architecturally, it denotes a stone, originally of similar shape, forming the topmost division of the capital of a classical column, and having the distinguishing features of a particular order.

In church architecture, Saxon, Norman, and subsequent styles have a distinctive form of abacus which often indicates age since it may be the only moulded part of the column. The diagrams give a general indication of the changes. Saxon (a) is generally flat and square: Norman (b) was at first square but later had a chamfered top and moulding: Early English (c) was generally circular and at times octagonal: Decorated (d) was either circular or octagonal, or polygonal: Perpendicular (e) was generally polygonal.

ABBEY

Low Latin *abbatio*, 'abbey'. Greek through Syriac *abba*, 'father'. The abbey is the group of buildings, or it is the group of men or women inhabiting those buildings, and named after the 'father' or head of the establishment, as a priory is named after the prior (q.v.) An abbot is equally head of a monastery as of an abbey, though 'abbey' suggests the communal life rather than the isolation of monastic life.

ABBOT

Ecclesiastical Latin *abbas*, 'abbot', Syriac *abba*, 'father'. Thus the meaning of the father or head of an abbey or monastery.

ACANTHUS

Latin, from Greek *akanthos*, from *akis*, 'thorn'. A type of thorn tree, the leaves of which were used as a model for decorating the capitals of Corinthian columns. The stylised form of the leaf is found wherever the classical influence prevails. (See 'Corinthian'.)

1

Adam is from Hebrew *Adama*, 'red' or 'red earth', referring to man's physical existence, and to the blood which is life to his body, and Eve is from Hebrew *Chavva*, 'mother of life'. The names are self-explanatory in the myth.

Representations of Adam and Eve show them as in the Genesis story, naked beneath the Tree of Knowledge, the serpent beguiling Eve, and Eve handing Adam an apple from that tree. The myth refers to the fall of Adam (that is, the other aspect of Adam – Man as a race of angelic beings androgynous by nature) to a life on the level of the senses with its attendant sexual split. The original bi-sexuality is suggested in the name itself, for in this interpretation 'Adam' can be seen to be composed of male and female elements, 'da' and 'ma'. The statement in Genesis is that Adam disobeyed God and ate of the Tree of Knowledge – he chose to experience the sensory world. The serpent symbolises the pride that lies at the root of his wilful separation from the Will of God and the cunning way it deludes him into a belief in his own importance: the forked tongue suggests this duality of belonging and separation, as it also suggests the duality inherent in the earth upon which, in the fallen state, he has to crawl. Both are naked, in the sense that the fall exposes Man to himself – to what he has done.

The serpent tempts Eve to eat of the apple and she is shown offering it to Adam. This is to say that Adam's female side, his feeling, intuition as pure Wisdom, knowing all things, is led into temptation, into time, where it becomes a separate female being. Separated in this way, his will is subject to the forces of the physical world and his soul is outside him. For this reason, in representations of the story, Eve is shown on Adam's left side. (See 'right and left'.)

Section of an

apple

The apple, which when cut in two reveals a five-pointed star denoting the five senses, as does the symbol of the fig-leaf in the myth, is the world itself, dependent upon physical generation; it is the fruit of the tree of error, and lodges between his head (the true source of power) and his fallen feelings and lower energies, in the form of the 'Adam's apple'. There is a hard lump here scarcely noticeable in woman – the price of eating is his division and a blockage to his power. Eve has fulfilled her function, because the life force is carrying on through propagation, and man has to find his will now through material experience, and by constant reference to Eve as his externalised soul. He can do this by seeing through the illusion proffered by the serpent, his pride, his ego that has lead him into error, and by giving back supremacy to his female side, pure Wisdom, so that once again he may be made whole – male-female. (See 'virgin'.)

AGNUS DEI

Latin, literally 'the Lamb of God', referring to Christ in his sacrificial role, and giving rise to the image of a lamb bearing a flag with a cross upon it. More specifically it denotes a small cake of wax stamped with this image and given to the faithful, a papal device of distributing the Paschal candle on the First Sunday after Easter. (See under 'lamb' for its symbolic aspects.)

AISLE

Latin *ala*, 'wing'. (The interposed 's' is due to the diminutive of *ala*, *ascella*.) The aisles in a church are the side divisions parallel to the nave, and separated from it by the pillars. The image of the two wings at the side of the bird is an obvious one, and the connection is perhaps better seen in the modern French *aille*, 'wing'.

Often aisles were built on either side of the nave in a church of simple design to give more space. When a single aisle was added it was on the north side because of the custom of burial on the south side.

ALABASTER

Greek *alabastros*, from the name of a town Alabastron in Egypt where the material was found and used. This stone, soft, white and semi-transparent, was mined and worked in Britain at Chellerston and Tutbury in the Nottingham area during the 14th century and became fashionable in the making of tombs and panels, finely carved and coloured with religious subjects. Reredos and retables (see under their respective headings) were also carved of alabaster with figures derived from the mystery plays of the period. The material was easily destructible and suffered much at the suppression of the monasteries.

ALB

Latin *albus*, 'white': and also seen in Old High German in *albiz*, 'swan', or 'white bird'. The alb is the whole girdled vestment worn by the priest during the celebration of the

3

mass, white in colour as a symbol of the purity of heart necessary in the communicant.

ALMONRY

Old English *aelmysse*, through Latin, through Greek *eleēmosunē*, meaning 'mercy, pity'. The almonry is the room in a monastic establishment used for the dispensing of food to the poor on certain days. It was a haven for those in distress and its presence kept alive the image of the connection between religion and charity. The room was located near the church or near the gate-house. The official dispenser of the alms was the 'almoner'.

ALMS-BOX

Old English *aelmysse*, through Latin and Greek (see 'almonry'). Alms-boxes, large oak boxes used for receiving offerings for the needy, are preserved in different parts of churches and cathedrals. (See 'chest'.)

ALPHA AND OMEGA

A and Ω are the capitals of the first and last letters in the Greek alphabet: they are constantly found in Church iconography with the meaning of the 'beginning and the end', as is also the Latin form *Initium et Finis*. They signify the beginning and end of the cosmic creative process. The connection with Christianity is through the statement in Revelation:

I am Alpha and Omega, the beginning and the ending, saith the Lord, which is, and which was, and which is to to come, the Almighty.

The sign Leo

The glyph A signifies the power of God as an initiating creative force, and can be seen either as a plough, the dividing compass, or the triangle of the Trinity raying downwards. In Ω lies the potential fulfilment of the teleological process. The word *omega* (o-mega) is literally the great 'o', as in English 'tone', to distinguish it from the short small *omikron* (o-mikron), the short 'o' as in English 'box'.

The glyph Ω can be seen not simply as a larger 'o' (as in the *omikron*) but one in which the ends of the circle are opened. This signifies the gaining of freedom, for the spiritual evolution of man is through the gaining of at-oneness with the Will of God: the small 'o', the circle of confinement in a material world has moved through to a release from that confinement. It is noticeable in this respect that the omega glyph

4

resembles the astrological sign Leo which has also much to do with self-authority.

The miniscule form of omega, ω, often replaces the capital, but is associated more with the Eastern Church. Its three co-joined arms suggest the final unifying in Man of the three aspects of the Trinity.

ALTAR

Low Latin *altar*, *altare*, 'altar' – originally a block of stone or wood upon which sacrifices by burning were offered.

The word was retained to denote the Christian altar, where there was a change of ritual if not of essential function. The ancient sacrifice of animals, representing the death of their corresponding natures within a man, gave way to the symbolic remembering of the sacrificial death of Christ; this was a death that, besides being an act of redemption for mankind, pointed to the need for each man to make his own sacrifice, to renounce his lower self, his animal nature. In the form of the medieval church, such a sacrifice is first indicated at the crossing – that is the area before the entry to the chancel where in pre-Reformation times the rood stood on the rood-loft (q.v.) or beam. This crucifix showed Christ suffering as man, and in those times dominated the approach to the eastern end of the church.

Properly, a communicant is not ready for entry behind the chancel without some stage in the path of sacrifice having been realised, for the altar is the place where the actual fruit of Christ's sacrifice, his 'body' and 'blood' are made available. Here, the sacrifice of Christ and the final surrender of a man's self-will to the Higher Will in him meet in one act. ('Sacrifice' is from Latin *sacer*, 'holy' and *facere*, 'to make'. 'Holy' and 'whole' come from the same Gothic root and in both words the meaning of healing is implied.)

Words connected with altar all suggest growth through change. Latin *altus* means 'high', so literally 'altar' is simply a raised structure, but it originally meant 'fully grown': the English word 'alter', from Latin *alterare*, 'to change', which is from Latin *alter*, 'the other of two', suggests that sacrifice is in fact a point of decision – in terms of the altar, a final break from the bonds of self.

In the early Christian church, altars were erected over places where relics of saints were kept, and when stone altars came to be used, the relics of saints were enclosed in them. The idea was thus committed to form that a tomb is really the place of

5

a new life: it is for this reason that the form of the altar is commonly adopted in the tombs to be found in graveyards of churches. Life has been yielded up, but the tomb or the altar is the place of transformation. Stone altars, common before the Reformation, gave way to the Holy Table, wooden and moveable if necessary, for the celebration of the Mass. Only a few original stone altars remain in this country. (See 'mensa'.)

ALTAR RAILS

There were no altar rails in England before the Reformation. The altar was then fenced off at the instruction of Laud to prevent its profanation. This was not a convenience for the communicants as now; in fact kneeling only became customary in the 13th century and before that there was an unbroken tradition of standing.

AMBULATORY

Latin *ambulare*, 'to walk'. A covered way in which to walk, as in a cloister, but especially denoting the area round the back of the high altar which is used as a processional way.

AMEN

Hebrew *amen*, 'so be it' or 'it is established', where the original Hebrew root means 'strength, stability'. As a termination to prayer currently and anciently used in Christianity, amen is a 'word of power', the key to which lies in the letters 'a' 'm' 'n'.

A–U–M

A–M–N

As a word of power, it is seen in ancient India as 'aum' or 'om' which expresses a fundamental duality in the God-head – male, father, initiator of action, in the letter 'a'; and female, mother, receptive substance in the letter 'm'. In between is a link, a solvent whereby the duality is made a unity, in the letter 'u'. These three aspects become in the one sound 'om', a symbol which embraces all that *is*, whether manifest or unmanifest.

In ancient Egypt the same duality 'a' and 'm' is seen in Amen or Amon, the name of the supreme Creator, the king of the Gods. (The root of the word means 'invisible'.) The letter 'n' adds the meaning of 'the issuing stream of life', a slightly different concept to the Hindus'. This is the word we have through Hebrew, Greek and Latin.

The meaning of amen lies in its actual sound value. 'A' is an open vowel sound representing outgoing creative energy; 'm' is a sound involving closure of the lips, and an almost total

6

containing of the reverberations within the body, representing the muteness and passivity of substance, the very antithesis of the 'a' sound; and 'n' involves opening the lips and by the placing of the tongue on the roof of the mouth, projecting the sound through the nose. This represents the continual issuing forth of intelligently ordered forms within that substance. This gives a trinity of Father, Mother and Son, A M N, embracing all that is in God and the world. (The letter 'e' signifies the vibrating field forces underlying all phenomena.)

Man not only lives in, but *is*, that whole process revealed in amen: 'man' is an anagram of the key letters, his plural is 'men', and the word 'name' is from all four letters. (Viewing man as a microcosmos, all things and their names are within man's comprehension.) As an intoned word, amen has effect upon the being of a man, building unity out of separated parts.

ANDREW'S CROSS or CROSS DECUSSATA

The cross with the arms intersecting diagonally is especially associated with St. Andrew. The same cross, the Greek letter *chi*, X, used in the monogram of Christ, had already been in existence for thousands of years, and is essentially a cross in spinning movement. It represents, like its variation the swastika in the diagram, the turning of the world and the setting in motion of creation. Man is inseparable from this act: all that is in the world is in him. This is hinted at in the fact that Andrew was the first disciple called by Christ and that the word Andrew derives from the Greek *andros*, 'man'. On another level, the story is that St. Andrew requested to be crucified on a cross of a form other than that associated with Christ, out of humility.

The cross is also called the 'cross decussata', from the Latin name for the numeral ten (X), from *decem*, 'ten'. Here the cross signifies all opposites embraced, for ten is the number of ordinal perfection, seen in the number 10, male and female, spirit and matter in one: the line of initiative and circle of receptivity are everywhere in mythology and life.

Heraldically, such a cross is a 'saltire cross', from Latin *saltarum*, 'stile', and *saltatorium*, 'stirrup', both from *saltare*, 'to leap'. The term is applied generally when two diagonal bands (called bends) cross on a shield.

ANGEL

Latin *angelus*, from Greek *angelos*, 'a messenger': cognate with a Sanskrit word *angiras* meaning 'divine being'. The function of the divine beings known as angels is that of messenger between God and man: in one sense they are superior to man since they are not bound by the finite world, and in another sense man is above the angels because his possibility is a growing towards his own divine nature, whereas angels are limited to their specific role.

According to early tradition (established by Dionysus the Pseudo Areopagite), there are nine orders of angels mediating between God and man – nine because of the squaring of the Trinity, representing the unfolding of man's powers in the three worlds, mind, heart and body, which can also be seen as spirit, soul and body.

For man this division denotes a spirit which is free, a body which is bound to earth laws, and an ensouling process giving a unique experience, the soul life of each man. There is a constant relationship between spirit and body, and a searching in his heart for values.

Correspondingly the angels have three major groupings, CHERUBIM, SERAPHIM and THRONES, relating to spirit; DOMINIONS, AUTHORITIES and POWERS relating to the soul; and PRINCIPALITIES, ARCHANGELS and ANGELS, relating to the level of the earth.

In art, Cherubims (divine knowledge) – Hebrew 'those grasped or held fast' – are depicted with heads full of eyes and two wings; Seraphims (divine love) – Hebrew 'those burning' – have the whole body and six wings, two above the face, two over the feet and two for flying. They are nearest to God and are aflame with love; Thrones (divine authority) – Greek *thronos* 'seat, throne' – have double wings and are portrayed supporting the throne of the Almighty and have heads fashioned according to the symbolical animals of the four fixed signs of the zodiac, which are also the symbols of the four Evangelists (q.v.). Thrones are also depicted as wheels without wings. All these, Cherubim, Seraphim and Thrones, have eyes both before and behind.

In the second group there is little attempt at defining exact function and portrayal in art. They are not easily represented because they stand for the Holy Spirit and the heart, but when they are, they have green vestments and hold a stave and a seal called the 'Seal of God'.

In the third group, Principalities control the laws governing the evolution of the earth; Archangels (Michael – judgement, Gabriel – mercy, Raphael – healing, and Uriel – prophecy are the chief ones) serve man as a whole; and Angels guide and protect men on the individual level. This third group is shown in art holding worldly weapons, musical instruments or tools of crafts, affirming their work of relating man to God on the earth level.

APOCALYPSE or REVELATION

Greek *apokaluptein*, 'to uncover, disclose', Latin *revelare*, from *re* and *velum* (veil), thus 'un-veiling'. The Apocalypse of John the Divine differs from the work of the four Evangelists whose aim was to establish the message of Christ on earth in such a way that it could be understood by men on all levels. Here on the contrary, by the uncovering of the veils of normal sensual awareness, John was granted a vision of spiritual realities so complex in symbolism as to protect them from profanation by literal understanding. Many of the archetypal images in the vision are found in iconography, especially the seven spirits before the throne, the Lamb, twenty-four elders, the dragon with the seven horns, the seven trumpets and the New Jerusalem.

In essence, the uncovering or unveiling is the story of the individual soul's spiritual awakening, the opening of seals of power within, leading to a complete perfecting and self-realisation. That the process is a complete one is signified by the frequent use of the number 7 – e.g., seven seals, seven thunders, seven churches, in addition to the ones already given. The individual soul, as in the ancient initiation ceremonies, is the hero (in this instance in the guise of the lamb or the rider of the white horse), victor over all the enemies within him, and these enemies are all the animal qualities epitomised in the 'dragon' and the 'beast' which have evolved through the aeons of time and oppose his inner growth. As in all myth, fairy-story and dream, in the astral world in this and the post-death state, and in initiation ceremonies, all the images and characters depicted are parts of his own being. Inversion of power is a common theme: the Lamb has become the beast; the bride, the harlot; and the New Jerusalem, Babylon. The process of regeneration is one of reversal and re-righting.

The four beasts around the throne are the same beasts associated with the Evangelists (q.v.). The four horsemen are controllers or reins of the types of energy related to those beasts and their respective elements. The white horse signifies equilibrated power. The seven churches symbolise the seven-fold division in the vast pattern of man's history, and, equally, subtle centres of power along the spine (*chakras*) found in ancient Yogic metaphysics; in both these senses, the churches can be seen as seven seals that one by one have to be unlocked. Such a complex symbolism, full of number puzzles, is like the parables, capable of interpretation on many levels, and need special study. (See 'lamb' and 'seven lamps'.)

APOSTLE

Greek *apostolos*, *apo*, 'away', and *stellein*, 'to send' – thus 'one sent forth, a messenger'. In the Christian reference, an apostle is one sent away to spread the message of the Gospel. Christ's twelve chosen disciples were the apostles deputed to do different areas of work in the world after his death: most suffered martyrdom. In fact, fourteen are customarily credited, twelve being the original disciples, with two additions, Matthias (chosen by lot to fill the place of Judas in the twelve) and Paul. The significance of the number fourteen lies in the fact that the fourteenth letter of the Hebrew alphabet signifies a fish; Christ was known as the Great Fish and much of early Christian symbolism is related to the Piscean era. (See 'fish' and 'piscina'.)

The fourteen disciples were sent into the deep sea of the material world to rescue souls to catch them for Christ. In church and cathedral they are profusely represented and are recognisable by their particular attributes or the circumstances of their martyrdom. The labels or scrolls the apostles carry contain the articles of one version of the Apostles' Creed to which each is said to have made his contribution before disbanding. (This tradition however only arose at the end of the 4th century.) The present form of the Creed was formulated in the 8th century but came directly from even earlier traditions. Paul and Judas are omitted, reverting back to the twelve. The following are some of the characterising features of the apostles in iconography: the appropriate article of an early form of the Creed is also given, together with the commonly found English version.

ST. PETER: traditionally has white hair and a short white beard, with a broad open face. He carries a bunch of keys because Christ gave him 'the keys to the kingdom of heaven'. Sometimes he is seen with a cock because of his denial of Christ, and sometimes with a chain which refers to the story of his imprisonment.

CREDO IN UNUM DEUM PATREM OMNIPOTENTEM CREATOREM COELI ET TERRAE (I believe in one God the Father Almighty, Maker of heaven and earth).

ST. ANDREW: is traditionally aged with white hair and beard. He carries the 'turning' or 'saltire' cross on which he was crucified (see 'Andrew's Cross').

ET IN JESUM CHRISTUM FILIUM EIUS UNICUM, DOMINUM NOSTRUM (And in one Lord Jesus Christ, the only-begotten Son of God).

ST. JAMES (MAJOR): is traditionally in mid-age with short hair and beard. He is the patron saint of pilgrims and is shown with a scallop shell, a pilgrim's staff, and a gourd.

QUI CONCEPTUS EST DE SPIRITU SANCTO NATUS EX MARIA VIRGINE (And was incarnate by the Holy Ghost of the Virgin Mary).

ST. JOHN: is traditionally young and without beard. John is shown with a cup which has a winged serpent flying out of it, with reference to the story that when John was challenged to drink poison he made the sign of the cross and Satan flew out of the cup in the form of a serpent. John then drank the contents of the cup unharmed. (See the similarity of this story with the role of John, and his common symbol of the eagle, discussed under 'Evangelists'.)

PASSUS SUB PONTIO PILATE, CRUCIFIXUS, MORTUUS ET SEPULTUS. (And was crucified also for us under Pontius Pilate. He suffered and was buried.)

ST. PHILIP: is traditionally young with or without beard. He carries a long staff topped by a cross because he died hanging from a long pillar: sometimes he carries a basket of loaves.

DESCENDIT AD INFERNOS, TERTIA DIE RESURREXIT A MORTUIS (He descended into hell and the third day he rose again according to the Scriptures.)

ST. JAMES (MINOR) or JAMES (THE LESS): is traditionally in mid-age with short hair and beard and resembling Christ due to the supposed blood relationship between them. Note the important article of the Creed afforded to him.

ASCENDIT AD CAELOS, SEDET AD DEXTERAM DEI PATRIS OMNIPOTENTIS (And ascended into heaven, and sitteth at the right hand of the Father).

ST. THOMAS: is traditionally young and without beard. He carries a builder's rule or sometimes the lance by which he was killed.

INDE VENTURUS EST JUDICARE VIVOS ET MORTUOS (And he shall come again with glory to judge both the quick and the dead).

ST. BARTHOLOMEW: carries a knife because he was flayed by one.

CREDO IN SPIRITUM SANCTUM (I believe in the Holy Ghost).

ST. MATTHEW: is traditionally an old man with a white beard. He is represented with a hatchet by which he was killed and often carries a money-bag indicating his trade as tax-collector. For an account of his role and symbol as evangelist see under 'Evangelist'.

SANCTAM ECCLESIAM CATHOLICAM; SANCTORUM COMMUNIONEM (And I believe one Catholic and Apostolic Church).

ST. SIMON: is traditionally old and with white beard. He carries the saw by which he was sawn to death.

REMISSIONEM PECCATORUM (I acknowledge one Baptism for the remission of sins).

ST. MATTHIAS: is traditionally old with white beard. He carries a battle-axe because he was beheaded by one.

CARNIS RESURRECTIONE (And I look for the Resurrection of the dead).

ST. THADDEUS (JUDE): is traditionally old with white beard. He is shown with the club by which he was killed, and sometimes carries a boat.

ET VITAM AETERNAM (And the life of the world to come).

JUDAS ISCARIOT: is represented with an ill-favoured countenance. He carries a bag because he was treasurer, and betrayer of spiritual values for money.

ST. PAUL: traditionally has a high forehead, long oval face and flowing beard. He carries a scroll denoting his epistles and a sword, because he was a fighter for the cause and died by the sword.

Latin *apsis*, from Greek *apsis*, 'arch' or 'vault'. Thus a semicircular or often polygonal projection at the eastern end of a church having a vaulted roof. The apse originated in the early churches that derived from the basilica, and remained more of a continental feature. Certain early English, Saxon and Norman churches have the apsidal shape at the eastern end – the crypts especially have retained this form under a changing superstructure. The eastern ends of English Gothic cathedrals are almost all square in shape.

ARCADE

Medieval Latin *arcata*, Latin *arcus*, 'bow'. A series of arches supported on columns, as in a cloister or ambulatory, but the term is more generally used to denote those found as decoration on the inside or outside of walls, and filled in with masonry.

ARCHANGELS

Greek *arkhos*, 'leader' and *arkhē*, 'beginning' (for 'angel', see under that heading). There are seven principal angels or archetypal spiritual beings whose habitation, according to Christian dogma, is before the throne of God, but of these only four are customarily singled out. (The significance of the number four is discussed under 'Evangelists'.) Their function is essentially mediation between the higher planes and man in his finite vehicle.

MICHAEL (Hebrew 'who is like unto the Lord') is found in the Bible narrative, and in iconography does battle with forces of evil. He is a patron of Christian warriors and is the defender of causes, so that in effigies of him he is clad in armour. As such he is a popular saint, as the immense number of churches in England and Wales dedicated to him show. On an inner level he could be seen as the real Self delivering the soul from the domination of the pseudo-self. He is also judge of the dead and is often represented with scales in which the soul of a man is weighed for judgement.

GABRIEL (Hebrew 'God is mighty') is the archangel of annunciation. He announces the future birth of John the Baptist to Zacharias, and of Christ to Mary. He is a messenger from higher planes to the earth level of a new inner birth of the spirit. In the Annunciation to the Virgin Mary he is represented as bearing a lily or an iris, the symbol of union between heaven and earth.

RAPHAEL (Hebrew 'healing of the Lord') is the dispenser of divine mercy to the sick, as in the story of Tobit. Raphael forewarned Adam of his situation. He is shown carrying a pilgrim's staff or a fish, a reference to the Tobit story.

URIEL (Hebrew 'flame of God') is an agent of prophecy in that he reveals the Will of God to man. He is seen with an open book or a spear.

ARCHITRAVE

Italian, from Greek *arkhos*, 'leader, chief', and Latin *trabs*, 'a beam'. Thus, chief beam. The lowest part of the entablature (q.v.) in classical architecture resting immediately upon the column.

ARMARIUM

Latin *armarium*, 'cupboard' (*arma*, 'arms, tools, implements'). Thus, a large cupboard in a cloister, or sometimes between the south door and the door of the chapter house, used for keeping books and materials for copying and illuminating.

ASCENSION

Latin *scandere*, 'to climb' – with *ad* we get *ascendere* and with *de*, *descendere*. The fact that *scandere* is cognate with Greek *skandalon*, meaning 'trap' or 'stumbling block', suggests the condition of any attempted ascent. In iconography, the Ascension is customarily represented by Christ ascending into clouds with only the lower part of the body or the feet showing, and the disciples looking up in awe. The looking up is the reverse image of the adoration of the shepherds looking down to the new-born child on the earth. The two images are the beginning and the end of empirical evidence of Christ on earth.

The Ascension, however, is followed by a final and most momentous occurrence – the descent of the Holy Spirit upon the apostles, described in Acts as tongues of flame, and so represented in art, showing that the Christ power was not lost by his disappearance from earth, nor was it a merely temporal phenomenon, but that it was a gift to the earth for all time – a special impulse in the evolution of Man.

The three key points of Christ's life, as represented in the

Church festivals, are reflected in the three key places in the plan of the church building. (See 'Crucifixion' and 'church'.) The birth (Christmas), is in the depths of winter, in the unawakened physical body; the spirit enters, and baptism symbolically enacts that birth at the foot of the church. The Crucifixion and Resurrection (Easter), are like the crossing in the church where the rood showing Christ suffering as man is seen. This point is to do with a re-righting in the life of the soul through sacrifice, the death of the passions and the lower mind. Easter is a moveable festival – it falls on the Sunday following the first full moon after the spring equinox, an indicator of the fact that cosmic forces enslave a man by the changing passions they engender. Sacrifice here gives rise to a gradual awakening and arising of the body from its old tomb; the body is now seen and used according to a new dawning in the understanding – the rising light of the sun suggested in the word 'Easter' which derives from a root meaning 'dawn'.

The third stage, the Ascension, followed by Whitsuntide or Pentecost, comes after a period of deprivation and strengthening – the forty days during which Christ revealed himself to the apostles. Such a stage is first a final release from all conditioning by materiality – a vision that reality is above the elements, that all is one spirit, one Man. This is the Ascension, and it is worthy of note that the word 'ascension' and others, 'scent', 'incense', 'sentience', all have the same association, (though they are said to be unrelated) of transcending material and rational values. (*Sentire* in Latin is both 'to feel' and 'to know'.) In the church this stage is reflected in the sanctuary containing the altar where the final joining or comm-union of all in one, is re-enacted. At such a stage a man bears his own fruit and has no more external reassurance.

The third stage culminates in Whitsuntide. The ten days are an agony of deprivation, but the number 10 symbolises the end of a perfectly whole process: now the Holy Spirit works through a man, using him as an instrument upon the earth where he was born. The fiery tongues are the same Holy Spirit that first announced the possibility of a new birth to Mary. The 'wit' in Whitsuntide is the pure wit of Higher Intelligence, also seen in 'white', and has a further root connection with Veda, the ancient sacred book of Hindus. At this level a man *knows* what to do without trying from himself. The earlier name 'Pentecost' means the 'fiftieth day' – that is the fiftieth day following the Sabbath after the Jewish Passover; but this gave way to the term Whitsuntide soon after the Norman Conquest.

The Ascension and Whitsuntide are then, the last act of a whole process of spiritual development, reflected in the form of the church and its rituals, starting with a re-birth from a dead husk of a materially orientated body and climbing back through many stumbling blocks to spiritual illumination – from west to east in the church. The ancient mysteries and initiations at one time brought about this ascent as it were, artificially, but Christ's sacrifice brought to each man the responsibility of his own 'I' consciousness – the power to make his own ascent.

ASS

Old English *assa*, and other Germanic forms, all from Latin *asinus*. The ass figures in Christian iconography by virtue of the fact that Christ rode into Jerusalem on this, the most lowly of animals. It is lowly because it is a beast of burden; and it is also stubborn and characteristically needs goading into action.

The ass symbolically is the burden of the physical world that the spirit has to bear and bend under. The inertias of that burden need to be broken through by the spirit within – the function of the goad. Christ rode on an ass indicating his readiness to take the burden of the errors of the world on his shoulders, and by voluntarily sacrificing his life, to redeem its direction. Man's spirit, once free, is now ignominiously confined in a material cage: the dark mark of the cross on the back and shoulders of the ass affirms that heavy burden. (See 'Nativity'.)

AUGUSTINIANS (or AUSTINS)

A monastic order founded in Chartres, differing little from the Benedictine Order, and so named through the traditional rule of the 5th century Augustine, Bishop of Hippo. They are an order of canons living under rule and having something of a halfway position between monks and secular clergy. Their houses came into Britain from 1105 and include Oxford, Bristol, Carlisle, and are the most numerous after the Benedictines. At the Suppression there were 170 houses.

AUGUSTINIAN (or AUSTIN) FRIARS

One of the four main orders of mendicant friars, founded in Italy in 1250 by Pope Innocent IV. They were in England by the same year.

AUMBRY or AMBRY (earlier word ALMARY)

Latin *armarium*, 'cupboard', *arma*, 'tools'. An aumbry is a small enclosed alcove, usually on the north side of the chancel, where the precious vessels of the Eucharist and the reserved sacrament are kept.

AUREOLE

Latin *aura*, 'gold', connected with *aurora*, 'dawn'. Thus, through the image of the radiating light of the sun at dawn, the aureole is the radiating mantle enveloping specifically the body as opposed to the head of a divine being. Mainly due to the needs of sculpture, it often becomes the 'vesica piscis' or 'mandorla', that is the elliptical shape drawn around the figure of the Almighty, Christ or the Virgin, always indicating glorification and apotheosis, and victory over the forces of evil. The generic term 'aureole', however, covers all forms of radiating light, varying according to the posture of the subject: very often it is circular when the figure is seated.

It came to be used more generally for the nimbus, the golden circle or disc of light surrounding the heads of saints, martyrs or any sacred figure. (See 'mandorla', 'glory', 'halo'.)

B

BALDACHIN

Baldachino, the Italian name for Baghdad. Originally, a baldachino was a canopy made of cloth from Baghdad, especially that canopy ritually carried over the Pope. It came to mean a structure of marble or stone on pillars, erected over an altar in a church.

BALUSTER

French *balustre*, 'small pillar', Latin *balaustium*, Greek *balaustion*, 'flower of the wild pomegranate'. The pillar was so named because of the shape of the flower; it is small, circular and swelling in the middle, usually supporting a handrail. Such pillars can occur in Norman churches as columns, but subsequently are only found in the 16th century with the influence of the Renaissance. The later and impure versions of the word are 'banister' and 'balluster'.

BALL-FLOWER

An ornament or moulding in the form of a round flower with three petals forming the cup. It belongs to the Decorated period of English architecture.

BANNER

An emblem of victory. The banner is an allusion to the conversion of Constantine who included his vision of the cross in his own banner. The banner is depicted along with the lamb as a symbol of victory over death. It says in fact, that he who dies to himself, lives. For this reason the banner is carried by Christ when he is depicted rising from the grave, or in his subsequent appearances on earth. Continuing the image of the lamb, John the Baptist is also shown with such a banner sometimes having upon it the words 'Ecce Agnus Dei' ('Behold the Lamb of God').

BAPTISTERY

Greek *baptisterion*, 'bathing place or swimming bath', *baptein*, 'to dip'. The baptistery is the part of the west end of a church where the font stands for the administering of the sacrament of baptism. The term was adopted by the early Christian Church because its ritual of baptism consisted of total immersion in water – until the year 1552 (the date of the second Prayer Book) children were dipped three times, first on the right side, then on the left and then with their face towards the font. In baptism lies the symbolic regeneration of a man, the washing away of error and the 'christening', that is the re-birth in Christ or en-Christing, denoted by the wearing of the chrisom (q.v.) by the child. For this reason a man is given a 'Christian' name – a new name for his new estate, originally, in the early Church, as an actual realised spiritual level, as opposed to his patriarchal name which refers simply to genealogical continuity.

The rituals of the Church however have undergone modification, and a further implication brought out through the ceremony taking place soon after birth, is that of baptism by fire, that is the fire of the Holy Spirit which is pre-figured in Christ's baptism by John the Baptist. In this, the dove, as elsewhere, appears as a symbol of the pure fire of the spirit. Thus the water in the font represents the immaculate womb – the possibility of man's emerging out of his fallen, material, vehicle back to a regenerated state through the power of the

Holy Spirit. This is connected with parables about the transformation of water, and with the words of Christ in John's gospel, 'Except a man be born of water and of the Spirit, he cannot enter into the kingdom of God'. For mention of the octagonal shape which figures in both baptistery and font, see under the heading 'font'.

BAROQUE

Portugese *barrocco*, 'an irregularly shaped pearl'. From this association, 'baroque' until the 19th century was a term meaning grotesque in design. Baroque was a style prevalent in roughly the 17th century, though in northern and western Europe it extended through the 18th century, involving the sculptor's use of strong curves and diagonals, and the painter's use of chiaroscuro (light and dark): the whole was intensely realistic. The Baroque leads into the Rococo. There is little true Baroque style in the architecture of Britain. Wren's St. Paul's in not wholly committed to the style and Vanbrugh's work is very individual.

BARREL VAULTING

The most simple kind of vault over a rectangular floor: also called a wagon-vault and also a cylindrical vault. The barrel vault was used classically and is found in Norman architecture. Also in Early English ceilings (basically a pointed arch where there was no stone vaulting), the frame produced the effect of the barrel vault.

BAR TRACERY

See 'tracery' and 'window'.

BASILICA

Greek *basileus*, 'king'. The original meaning was of a king's throne room, but in Roman times it came to mean a hall for the administration of justice. Such a hall was a simple oblong shape with a rounded semi-circular end (apse) where a tribunal sat. In front of the tribunal was an altar for sacrifices. The early Roman Christians adapted their needs to this form, giving an entrance chamber or narthex, a nave and an apse with an altar.

The basilican-form church was introduced into Britain along with the missionary enterprises of St. Augustine, and was largely confined to the south east (for instance St. Pancras at Canterbury), though crypts at Ripon and Hexham (circa

Apse

Altar

Nave

Narthex

670) are part of what were basilican-type churches. After the 7th century, the form gave way to the indigenous Celtic style – a square presbytery, tall west tower and transepts. A return to the basilican form after the Conquest was short-lived.

BASILISK

Latin *basilicus*, 'a kind of lizard', thus a kind of serpent, Greek *basiliskos*, 'a little king,' *basileus*, 'king'. As a fabulous creature depicted in art it has the body of a cock and a tail made of three serpents. Its glance was said to kill and it could only be conquered by holding a mirror before it, when, frightened at its own image, it burst. In Christian art, the basilisk is an embodiment of evil. Psychologically, evil is disempowered when it is seen face to face.

Clerestory

Triforium

Arcade

BAY

French *baie*, 'an opening', from a word *bayer*, 'to gape', now in disuse.

A bay is one of the compartments into which the nave of a church is divided, and the term is also applied to divisions in the roof. In a cathedral the bay is composed of three levels, arcade, triforium and clerestory, one above the other. The function of the arcade is to take the strain from above with the minimum of support, i.e. in the piers; of the clerestory to let light in; and of the triforium, as with all middle areas, to balance and link higher and lower to form a living whole.

BEAK-HEAD

An ornament in Norman doorways which has the shape of a bird's beak, hooked, and projecting downwards.

BELFRY

Middle English *berfray*, from Old French *berfroi*, from Latin *berfridus*: a Germanic loan word – Middle High German *bercfrid*, 'a watch tower'. This is in turn from two German words: *bergen*, 'to protect' and *frit*, 'a place of security'.

Bells were hung in watch towers as alarms, and the original meaning gradually gave way to a stress on the bells themselves: thus the change of the word.

BELL

Old English *belle*, related to Dutch *bel*, 'bell'. The Old English word *belen* is 'to bellow'.

On one level the bells of the Middle Ages were a part of

life, as time-keepers, used for festive occasions and for inform-
ing the people of emergencies. But on another level there is
also the power of the bell: its repeated sounding is remini-
scent of the repetition of a mantra or prayer. Bells have
always had an important place in the Church – upon their
installation they were blessed, for their true function was to
banish evil and disharmony. In the early Irish Church the
bell was second only to the Book in the insignia of the Saints,
and it had magical powers and was handed down from generation to generation for safe preservation.

The bell (the word itself can be seen as the word 'be' and
el – Hebrew for God) represents the power and beauty of
the heart of God – the very Being of God. A will which has
become pure by resignation to the Will of God is both powerful and beautiful: we find this paradox indicated in the inversion, from Latin *bellum*, 'war', to French *belle*, 'beautiful'.
Using its true power, the bell draws people from their worldly
pursuits, proclaiming the moment when the host is raised for
adoration, or sounds the solemn note of the relinquishing of
the individual will at death. On a psychological level, each
man aiming to find his own pure being has a particular function and name: so too does a bell receive a name when it
makes its first sound.

There is a tradition which says that bells in the Church were
first used in Campania, a district in central Italy, thus giving Low Latin *campana*, 'bell', and the word *campanile*, 'bell-
tower'.

BENEDICTINES

A monastic order founded at the beginning of the 16th
century by St. Benedict, who was the first to introduce Eastern
monasticism to the West. Some of the rules observed were
poverty, celibacy, spare diet, industry and 'stability', that is
residence in one place for life. The Benedictine rule was the
first in this country to break the arbitrariness of monastic discipline. They were known as Black Monks. The older monasteries in Britain are Benedictine, and included Westminster, Canterbury, Peterborough, Whitby. At the time of
the Suppression of the Monasteries there were 276 Benedictine
houses.

BIBLE

Latin *biblia*, Greek *biblia*, 'collection of writings' – both
from an Egyptian loan word *biblos*, 'the pith of papyrus'. The

Latin singular *biblia* signifies the Book of all books, but the Greek word *biblia* is a plural noun signifying the collection of books on papyrus rolls upon which the writings were found.

The Bible is in two parts. To people of New Testament times, the Old Testament was referred to as the Holy Scriptures. The Old Testament concerns the covenant made by Moses to which the people of Israel failed to adhere, thus giving their sense of despair. The New Testament tells of a new covenant, redeeming the old, which was brought about by the incarnation of God as man in Jesus Christ.

The Old Testament, written in Hebrew, was essentially in three parts, drawn together circa A.D. 90 along with a fourth book added at a relatively late date. It consisted of: the Pentateuch (literally 'made of five books'), mainly The Law; the Prophets, mainly prophetic material; the Writings, all other books not included in the first two sections; and the fourth part, now called the Apocrypha.

The first Christian writings forming the New Testament are those of St. Paul about the middle of the 1st century with the four Evangelists following later in the century. It was not until the middle of the 2nd century however that there was reference to the Gospels as a whole unit. Though Jews of Palestine were bi-lingual, the mother tongue was largely Greek, not Aramaic, and the Gospels were written on papyrus in Greek, the earliest dating from the 3rd and 4th centuries. Only in the 4th century do we find a whole New Testament, and there are only two examples, known as Codex Siniaticus and Codex Vaticanus.

Due to such variable sources, versions made by the Latin Church were becoming more and more numerous and inaccurate, and it was St. Jerome who, late in the 4th century, revised the New Testament and finally translated the whole of the Old Testament into Latin (the Latin language was then the unifying agent of Europe) using original Hebrew manuscripts. This version, the Vulgate, an abbreviation of *vulgato editio*, 'popular edition', from *vulgus*, 'multitude', remained the parent of all Western European bibles for many centuries. In the 8th and 9th centuries translations were made from the Latin in Britain, as in the added word-for-word text in the Lindisfarne Gospels, but these were mostly partial and it was Wycliffe's Bible (14th century), the work of five scholars, that gave the first whole translation into English. In Europe as a whole the theological influence of Luther led to many translations from the Latin and Greek. The versions of Tyndale, Coverdale and the so-called Great, Geneva, and Bishop's (Rheims) Bibles were in this tradition, and led to the Authorised Version, known as the King James Version, in 1611. This was carried out by forty-seven scholars with instructions to use the previous versions of the 16th century where necessary, and in particular, large parts of Tyndale's translation, were used.

However, in considering the translations of the Bible certain facts are worthy of note: that the original text was in Greek uncials or capitals (see 'uncial'); that transmission by manuscript was prone to error and embellishment; that there were no breaks shaping words into sentences, nor was there any division into chapter and verse. (Chapters are found for the first time in the Latin bible printed in Paris in the 13th century, and verses were used first by the Parisian typographer-royal, Stephen, in the 16th century.) These were contributory factors to the difficulty of interpretation – whether a sentence was interrogative or not, for instance – facing the early translators, and the Authorised Version could be said to have had only three major printed versions in Latin or Greek at its disposal: the first printed bible in Latin in 1462; that in Greek in 1514 by Cardinal Ximenes along with a Latin translation, known as a 'polyglot'; and Erasmus' version of 1516. The Parisian typographer Stephen produced a version almost identical with Ximenes and Erasmus, and Walton's 'polyglot' of London 1600, used Stephen's edition. (See 'book' for the wider issues of the 'Book of Life' and 'Breeches Bible'.)

BISHOP

Old English *biscop*, Old High German *biscof*, Latin *episcopus*, Greek *episkopus*, 'overseer'. (From *epi*, 'over' and *skopos*, 'a watcher'.) Thus one who presides over a particular area being colonised in the early Church. (See 'cathedral'.)

BLAZON

Old French *blason*, 'shield' and 'coat of arms', Middle English *blazon*, 'shield', connected with German *blasen*, 'blow' or 'proclaim'. In this sense it is the same proclamation of a man's lineage as is in the word 'herald'. It has come to mean more specifically the accurate description of the arms – to blazon is to paint and inscribe a shield with appropriate arms. Until the 15th century French words were used, then English blazonry used its own adopted words. The order in the science was: first the 'tincture', that is the colour of the 'field' or background, then the main 'charge', that is the object on that field and its tincture, then other lesser charges. Blazonry is based on the sharp contrast between the field and the charges: for instance a gold or silver field (called 'metal') would have a pure red, blue, black or purple charge.

BLESSING

Old English *blēdsian*, 'to bless, consecrate', from a German root *blod*, 'blood'. The idea inherent in the word is that of sacrifice through the shedding of blood, and is also seen in the French *blesser*, 'to wound'. Shedding of blood, fusing, and drinking blood are part of many primitive rituals.

God's sacrifice is the shedding or diffusing of His power in the act of creation, a self-inflicted wound which culminates on the physical plane in the shedding of the blood of Christ to redeem man. The blessing in the Latin Church is a symbolic purification of man's impure blood in the name of the Trinity, in the sense that the blood is the mediator between the spirit and the body. The state of the blood corresponds to his inner state, so that, for example, when his animal nature is aroused, his blood 'rises'. The purification takes place on the three levels of the Trinity (Father, Son, Holy Ghost), respectively in the will, the thinking and the feeling; it is symbolised by the three first fingers of the raised right hand, itself the hand of power. The thumb (Father) is the finger that wilfully crushes down, the index finger (Son) directs and points in judgement, and the second finger (Holy Ghost) is the one used for tactual reference representing the feeling life and, on the lowest level, sensuality.

When the hand is seen giving the Benediction with the third finger touching or crossing the thumb, and the others either erect or curved (b and c), the Eastern Orthodox Church is indicated. (The break between East and West occurred technically in 1054 though there was overlapping of imagery.) There are two known suggestions for the emerging of this gesture. It is said that the fingers spell out by their shape, and in sequence, the letters IC XC, the first and last letters of the Greek words 'Ιησους Χριστος, Jesus Christ. In the other, the erect little finger gives I, the thumb crossing the third finger gives X, and the slightly separated index and second finger gives 'v', the first letters of the words 'Ιησους Χριοτς νικα, 'Jesus Christ conqueror'. In each case, however, the enclosure made by the thumb and the ring finger (the fourth of the five fingers) denotes the value of existence in the ring of physical existence, with special reference to the birth of Christ on earth. (See 'cross'.)

BOND

A variant of 'bind', found in all Germanic languages, meaning 'to tie up'. In building, the term denotes the way that stones or bricks overlap in the building of a wall. In Flemish bond the 'header' showing its end, and the 'stretcher' showing its side, alternate, whereas in English bond, used between 1560 and 1700, the alternation was by layer.

BOOK

Old English *boc*, 'document', from a Germanic stem meaning 'beech-tree'. Old Norwegian also has *boc*. The word 'book' is derived from the custom of inscribing letters on pieces of beechwood in temperate regions. The 'Book of Books', the Bible, was of course written on parchment scrolls.

But both the scroll and the book are to do with unfolding of life, both in terms of the individual and the human race. The scroll suggests this visually, whilst the book, deriving from the eternally self-generating tree, the tree of life, shows the progression page by page. All references to 'book' in the Bible indicate lineage and unfolding. In iconography the Book is held for this reason in the left hand of God the Creator, Christ in Majesty, or of any of the Evangelists – physical generation, in one sense equatable with evil, is always symbolised by the left side. (See 'right and left' and 'devil'.)

The Latin *liber*, 'book', also has this connotation, for its original meaning is 'inner bark of a tree', since this was used for writing on, and pieces collected together formed a book. *Liber* also means 'free' – in the present sense something has been liberated: here is the Book of Life again. But *Libra* (etymology said to be uncertain), a pair of scales and the name of the constellation Libra, signifies a weighing in the balance and at the half-way mark of the zodiac suggests the crisis point of backwards or forwards. Such a point is the key to both the Book of Life of man as set out in the Bible and to an individual's own book of life.

In this sense the creation of Genesis led to a dark point of despair, the crucial material midpoint, where an impulse had to be sent to the earth in the form of the descent of God as man, making possible a return from despair to hope and a new spiritualised condition. This is in fact a statement of the descent from higher planes into a physical body and an ego structure, a fall that can be redeemed by the 'I' consciousness, that is the positive side of the ego – the Christ in me – which can transform previous fallen stages. In terms of one human life, the fall to the depths is from childhood innocence to the rational pride and egotism of middle years, and a return through a re-birth to the wisdom of old age.

$$Spirit \longrightarrow \begin{matrix} Body \\ Ego \end{matrix} \qquad Spirit$$

Innocence   I conciousness   Wisdom

       ⟵ Possible directions ⟶

Old Testament ⟶ Birth of Christ   New Testament

The Fall   New Jerusalem

The question however is whether the crucial new birth will be allowed to develop: the possibility has been opened up, but each man has to make his choice. The Book, the Bible, reveals the possibility of such a birth and a return through emulation of the life of Christ as shown in the New Testament. The Birth, Crucifixion, Resurrection and Ascension are to be seen as stages in inner transformation. The fact that this is a retracing and a re-righting of a downwards movement typified in the despair of the Old Testament is indicated by the many obvious correspondences between the Old and the New Testaments.

The final chapter in the Book is the one of judgement, because a man's 'book of life' will ultimately be laid bare to him: such a book is referred to in the Apocalypse. (See 'Last Judgement'.) In iconography, a book held by an evangelist or apostle is the New Testament, and more generally symbolises the learning of the saints. (See 'Bible' for historical aspect.)

BOOK OF HOURS

A prayer book for the laity consisting of prayers used for private worship, and reaching popularity in the 15th century. The calendar is illustrated by the Occupations of the Month, and the life of the Virgin is illustrated in eight miniatures according to the canonical hours (q.v.) as follows:

The Annunciation – to Matins
The Visitation – to Lauds

The Nativity – to Prime
The Annunciation to the Shepherds – to Tierce
The Presentation in the Temple – to Nones
The Flight into Egypt or the Massacre of the Innocents –
to Vespers
The Coronation of the Virgin or the Flight into Egypt –
to Compline

The quality of the work varied because of the enormous numbers made, but some of the finest illuminated manuscripts are among them.

BOSS

French *bosse*, 'lump, knob'. A boss is the projecting ornamental carving found at the intersection point of ribs and ceilings, or at the end of weather-mouldings above doors and windows. In the Norman vaults they are rarely found; in the Early English period ceilings have carved bosses mostly of foliage and occasionally small figures; in the Decorated period foliage, animals, and heads are found; in the Perpendicular period there is an abundance of armorial bearings.

BRASSES or SEPULCHRAL BRASSES

The first brass engravings on tombstones appeared at the end of the 13th century, mostly on slabs in the pavement in the church but sometimes raised as altar tombs. The alloy metal used was called latten and was originally embedded in pitch and fastened by rivets, the incised lines being filled with a resinous substance.

In Britain separate pieces of brass such as the inscription and canopies were inset about the whole stone whereas on the continent the whole engraving was done on one rectangular piece of brass. The images illustrate the many changes in armour of the knights of the period. By 1400, different social classes were adopting brasses as monuments, and from the Lancastrian period (1400-53) about 500 brasses are known to exist. From 1453 to 1485, in the Yorkist period, the engraving deteriorates in quality and from the Tudor period up to 1547, 2,000 brasses remain of varying quality.

Monumental brasses suffered at the Dissolution of the Monasteries and in 1537 when church plate was confiscated, many brasses were removed for melting down. Some brasses were, however, re-engraved by using the reverse side or by simply altering the existing figures: such brasses are known as 'palimpsest' (q.v.). During the reigns of Elizabeth and James I (d. 1625) few brasses were laid down and many were fixed to walls. The deterioration continued in the Caroline period up to 1660.

BREECHES BIBLE (THE GENEVA BIBLE)

A bible often seen in show-cases of churches, and so-called because the word breeches was in this particular bible substituted for the fig-leaf in the story of Adam and Eve in Genesis.

In other respects it was an important landmark in the translation of the Bible into English. Published in Geneva in 1560 by William Whittingham with the aid of two others, it was the first to have ordinary roman type, the first to have chapters divided into verses, and also the first to use italics for words whose purpose was merely to explain and connect in order to clarify meaning, though both of these latter innovations had already been made in other tongues earlier in the 16th century.

BREVIARY

Latin *breviarium*, 'summary', from *brevis*, 'short'. A book, used by priests, containing Divine Office for each day: it is usually in the form of one book for each season.

BULL

Middle English *bule*, *bole*, Middle High German *bulle*, from a base meaning 'to swell'. The bull, the fixed earth sign of the zodiac (Taurus) is the symbol of St. Luke in Christian iconography. The idea behind the fixed signs is that of the establishment of power on the physical plane via the elements, and the Evangelists established the message of Christ in the world, each in his own way corresponding to one of these modes of activity. The element 'earth' in its 'fixed' state is connected with phallic power and sexual secretion – hence the root 'to swell' and the connection of the bull with the throat. (See 'Adam and Eve'.)

The other three fixed signs of the zodiac and their corresponding animals and Evangelists are: Aquarius (air sign) – man, Matthew; Leo (fire sign) – lion, Mark; Scorpio (water sign) – eagle, John. The eagle 'Aquila' is an extra-zodiacal sign substituted symbolically. (See 'Evangelists'.)

BUTTERY

Old French *boterie*, from *boutellerie*, 'the place where bottles are kept'. In a monastery it is the store place for wine and ale, and the place from which they were dispensed. (Thus the modern office of 'butler' as dispenser of drink.)

BUTTRESS and FLYING BUTTRESS

Old French *bouterez*, from *bouter*, 'thrust, push'. The characteristic of the soaring medieval cathedral is the need to counter-balance the outward thrust of the high vaults. Such a counter-thrust begins with the delicate 'flying' buttress, immediately opposite the vault, which joined increasingly heavier support in its descent to the ground. (See 'Gothic'.)

'Flying'

C

CALEFACTORY

Latin *calefacere*, 'make hot', from *caleo*, 'be hot' and *facere*, 'to make'. The term used in referring to a monastic establishment denotes the underground room containing the large bricked fireplace used for general heating purposes.

CAMBER

Latin *camera*, 'arch, vault', Greek *kamara*, 'any construction with a vaulted or arched roof': the roots mean 'bent'. Thus in architecture, a slight curve on a surface: it also denotes the slope of a beam in a roof, such as a tie-beam.

CAMERA

Latin *camera*, 'vault, arch', Greek *kamara*, 'any construction with a vaulted roof'. The word also came to be 'chamber' through Old French *chambre*, from the same root.

'Camera' when used in referring to a monastic building, is used in the same sense as 'chamber' – that is the special anteroom or private room of a dignitary.

CANDLE

Latin *candela*, 'tallow-candle', *candere*, 'to glow, burn'. The significance of the candle in Church ritual derives historically from the words in Revelation XI – 'These [referring to two witnesses] are the two olive trees and the two candlesticks standing before the Lord of the earth.' The olive tree and its oil symbolise love (see 'Christ' and 'oil') and the candle, with its light, the power of 'wisdom' to illuminate the human soul.

Oil, psychologically love, and the candle, the light of wisdom, are both inherent in pure being, and man has fallen away from pure being towards egotism, hate, intellectual pride, and erroneous knowledge. The candle is traditionally made of bees' wax, and the life pattern and nature of the bee is essentially to do with pure being. It makes honey, which has always been a symbol of spiritual truth, all is centred around the queen, representative of female Sophia or Wisdom, and it gathers the purest essence of flowers. Again, significantly, the males are killed by the females once their function is over: this is not to say that the male process, away from pure being towards intellection and egotism, is without value – it is an inevitable process which must follow through to its term. But the light of pure being, the candle, eternally wise, shines in man's temporal temple eternally, and this is what has to be recovered if he is not to go downwards irrevocably. In this respect there is a three-fold process – a state of innocent wisdom, a movement away from this to error and separateness, and the light still living beneath that error finally bursting forth to give a new wisdom through experience. (See 'book'.)

CANON

Latin *canonicus*, 'one subject to rule or canon'. Greek *kanon*, 'straight rod, carpenter's rule'. Greek classical authors were referred to as *kanones* because they were models of perfection in their conformity to rule. Hence all the meanings: a rule set by the Church; or in 'canon law' the whole system of Church law recognised by civil authority before the Reformation; a Church dignitary.

CANONICAL HOURS

The word canonical is from the Greek *kanon*, 'a straight rod' and 'a standard of excellence': and further back from *kanna*, 'reed'.

The Canon is thus the system of Church law in Western Europe prior to the Reformation, and the canonical hours are the hours of prayer standardised by the Benedictines and laid down in monastic institutions. Originally the order was: Nocturnes, Lauds, Prime, Tierce, Sext, Nones, Vespers, Compline. Nocturnes (night) and Lauds (praise at daybreak) however came to be joined into one Matins (morning), giving seven canonical hours.

MATINS: ecclesiastical Latin *matutinus*, from *Matuta* 'Goddess of Morning' (whence the associated word *maturus*, 'mature'). Within the period 12 to 3 a.m.

PRIME: Latin *primus*, 'first', because the first hour of daylight. Period from 3 to 6 a.m. but now fixed at 6 a.m.

TIERCE: Latin *tertius*, 'third', because the third hour of the day. Period 6 to 9 a.m. but fixed now at 9 a.m.

SEXT: Latin *sextus*, 'sixth', because the sixth hour. Period 9 to 12 noon and now fixed at 12 noon.

NONES: Latin *nonus*, 'ninth', because the ninth hour after 6 a.m. Period between 12 and 3 p.m., now fixed at 3 p.m.

VESPERS: Latin *vesper*, 'evening' – that is 6 p.m.

COMPLINE: Latin *completa*, 'completed'. The last service in the day in the remaining period between 6 and 12 p.m., around 9 p.m.

The seven periods have been related to the crucial times in the Passion of Christ; for instance, condemnation to death (Tierce), Crucifixion (Sext), gives up the Ghost (Nones). In the 'Book of Hours' they are related to the significant phases in the life of the Virgin Mary, and they have also been related to the sequence Christmas, Lent, Easter, Ascension (Matins, Prime, Tierce, Sext). Or they may be equally seen as six periods followed by one, completing the seven days of creation.

The services, not practicable for parochial congregations, were joined at the Reformation to give a morning service and an evensong.

CANOPY

Latin *canopeum*, from Greek *konopein*, 'gnat'. *Konopein* is a combination of *konos*, 'cone-shaped', and *ops*, 'eye' or 'face' – descriptive of the shape of a gnat's head. A canopy is a cone-like structure of wood or stone erected over a pulpit, font or sedilia in a church, taking its name from such a shape. The constructions vary according to the style of the period, those of the Early English period being simple in form with the Decorated and Perpendicular ones being worked in greater detail.

CAPITAL

Latin *caput*, 'head' (the genitive case is *capitis*), Sanskrit *kapalum*, 'skull'. The head of a column in architecture. In the great English periods – Norman, Early English, etc. – the capital clearly indicates the age of the work. Norman capitals are diverse, Early English are devoid of carving, simple or of

Over a pulpit

Norman   Early English   Decorated   Perpendicular

Doric   Ionic   Corinthian

bold clear foliage, and in the Decorated period the foliage is much more complex and representational. In Perpendicular work, capitals are often polygonal and plain with less pronounced mouldings and, when foliage is used, it is stiffer in quality. In classical tradition there are three major forms of capital (see 'column' and 'order') – Doric, Ionic and Corinthian.

CARMELITES

One of the four main orders of mendicant friars (relying upon alms for support), taking their name from Mount Carmel in the Holy Land where the order was founded by St. Berthold the Crusader. They were expelled by the Saracens in the 13th century and came into Europe. In the 15th century St. Theresa the Spanish mystic founded an austere discalced branch. ('Discalced' means literally 'de-shoed' – but in the order either barefoot or in sandals.)

CARTHUSIANS

A monastic order founded about 1086 by St. Bruno, and taking its name from the original monastery at Chartreuse (Latin *Cartusianus*) near Grenoble, France. The order was extremely ascetic and its architecture severe. Speech was forbidden and each monk ate and worked in the solitude of his own cell around the cloister. At the Suppression there were eight Carthusian houses in Britain.

CARTOUCHE

Italian *cartiocco*, Latin *carta*, 'leaf of paper or papyrus', Greek *khartēs*, 'leaf of papyrus'. Following the Egyptian meaning of an oval shape bearing the title of a king, a cartouche has come to mean a tablet, enclosing an inscription, usually with an ornate frame. They are frequently to be found on tombstones and commemorative plaques.

CATHEDRAL

Greek *kathedra*, 'seat' : *kata*, 'down to' and *hedra*, 'seat' – thus 'a seat to sit down on'. A cathedral is a church with a bishop's seat or throne, and thus a symbol of authority within the structure of the Church: the name 'cathedral' became applicable only when an establishment had been endowed with a bishopric. The same seat is found also in the Latin language, for the 'see' of the bishop derives from *sedes*, 'seat'. The throne itself is found in the stalls of the choir, distinguishable by its size and the richness of its carving. The power of the bishop was originally in the nature of head of a family of clergy, but the growth of the chapter, exercising power over property, finance, and most Church affairs, caused his position to become an increasingly honorary one. The loss of the original function is now compensated by the responsibility for a diocese.

Architecturally, the cathedrals and monastic churches of Western Europe were at first similar in design to the Roman basilica where the tribunal presided in the apse with the altar in front of it. The bishop's throne was in the centre of the apse, where the clergy also sat, with the altar and singers to the west of them. Gradually the monks' choir came to be enclosed by screens, and the transepts were moved westwards. Variations of form in time and place were however inevitable. In England, even as late as the time of the great cathedrals, in order to provide services for laymen and monks, the east end was often modified to become as long as the nave, a factor which contributed to the dignified length of the English cathedral. It is an interesting point, too, that the building of a cathedral was always started from the east end, and progressively moved westwards. If this is borne in mind whilst looking at the present day building, confusion through the mixing of styles can often be avoided.

Seen from an 'inner' point of view, the early church was a place of inner teaching, open only to those undergoing initiatory instruction, different parts of the building having significant relationship to attained levels. As the church opened to the people certain inner truths were inevitably lost. Nevertheless, their essential meaning was still held and disguised in the form and contents of the church, especially in the cross which had established itself as the symbol of Christianity. In the medieval period, the cruciform cathedral was taken by the religious zeal of the time and thrown upwards into vertical vaults and spires. The attempt to reach heaven was the cause of drastic changes in architectural techniques: upward thrust needed balancing against downward pressure, insubstantial aspiration against substantial reality, fire against earth. Thus the cathedral became a finely balanced instrument with the two forces reconciled in a third force, its perfect art form.

As a living entity, priesthood and people were similarly side by side, the mystery of the sanctuary balanced by the workaday nave where worship, festivity, education, and craft were carried out. In short, the cathedral represented the soul of the people, and its form a unique balance between earth and heaven. (See 'Gothic'.)

CATHOLIC

Greek *katholikos*, 'universal'. *Kata* is 'according to' and *holos*, 'entire, whole'. The term originally denoted the Holy Catholic Church, embracing all Christians in one body, and after the Reformation it denoted all those Christians under the jurisdiction of the Pope, as opposed to the Reformed, Protestant Church. The Catholic Church in this sense claims true universality through an unbroken tradition from Christ himself, a universality until recently affirmed by the use of Latin throughout the world.

CELLAR or CELLARIUM

Latin *cella*, 'store-room or granary hut', Greek *kalia*: this is from a root meaning 'to hide or conceal' whence Latin *celare*, 'to hide' and the English 'conceal'. The origin of this connection between words must have been the safeguarding of food in times of invasion. In a monastery the cellars are the provision rooms superintended by a cellarer.

34

Latin *Celta* and Greek *Keltoi*. The Aryan-speaking race known as Celts included the ancient Gauls, and inhabited a large area of Western Europe. The Bretons, Scottish Gaels, Welsh, Cornish, Irish and Manx are all consequent upon the migrations of this race.

In pagan Europe, before Christ, the bronze work shows a high degree of skill and was typified by the use of spiral curves. There was no attempt at realistic representation and the few speciments of animal forms are conventionalised. With the advent of Christianity into Ireland, bringing an unprecedented flowering of decorative art, there were inevitable modifications. The Irish Celts had an inventiveness and precision which found expression in interlacing circles, key patterns and knot patterns. The spiral ornament of the illuminated manuscripts, as in the Book of Kells and the Irish sculptured crosses of the 7th to 10th centuries, is the greatest achievement of Celtic Christian art. Irish monasticism, spreading to Northumbria, brought a marriage of it and the native style to give such manuscripts as the Lindisfarne Gospel-book. It carried on the tradition of sculpture in Irish-Saxon sculptured stones.

CEMETERY

Latin *cemeterium*, Greek *koimētērion*, 'consecrated ground for burying the dead'; from words meaning 'lying down, sleeping, bed, place to lie'. In medieval life the term implied the graveyard attached to the parish church. The word now denotes any consecrated ground separated from a church.

CENSER (also called THURIBLE)

Latin *incensum*, 'something burnt'; thus the vessel made of gold, silver or brass which hangs by chains and burns incense during the Church rituals. Thurible is from Latin *thus*, 'frankincense' and Greek *thyos*, 'a sacrifice', suggesting early sacrificial rituals.

CENTAUR

A mythical half-horse, half-man creature, from Greek *Kentauros*, a member of a race of Thessaly. It was the centaur Chiron who, through being teacher of music, medicine and hunting to many heroes, was placed by Jupiter in the heavens, to become the constellation Sagittarius: here he represents

On a misericord, Exeter

essentially the power of the horse plus the wisdom of man, and is represented with bow and arrow (Latin *sagitta*, 'arrow'). In medieval times the centaur was called the Saggitary, and in Norman fonts and carved doorways he is seen with bow and arrow in contest with monsters, denoting the conquest of the flesh by harnassed spiritual power.

CHALICE

Latin *calix*, Greek *kalyx*, 'cup, outer vessel of a flower or bud'. In the Church ritual the chalice is the cup used to contain the wine in the celebration of the Eucharist. As such it represents the chalice of the Last Supper referred to in the New Testament, and in the original Roman ritual, by the words:

> Take and drink ye all of it. For this is the chalice of my Blood of the new and eternal testament . . .

It is also the supposed receptacle of the blood of Christ at the crucifixion, in which association it becomes known as the Holy Grail.

The historical controversy centering around Joseph of Arimathea and the Holy Grail is not within the scope of this book. What is essential to the chalice, the Grail, and the drinking of the 'blood of Christ', is the quest for purity. The chalice is a female image, a container, primarily of the waters of existence; it is also the container of the wine which is the re-spiritualised waters. That wine is symbolic of the blood of Christ, for it is in partaking of this blood that man may return to the source of Wisdom. The derivation of the word itself (see also 'ciborium') suggests the perfected essence at the heart of the flower.

36

The ritual of partaking of the blood is based on the fact of the blood being the mediator between the spirit and the physical body: in this sense, in a perfected being such as Christ, the blood would be expunged of impurity. The drinking of the blood of higher beings, here, and in primitive rituals has always had the purpose of taking in the power of that being.

As the chalice is female, so the spear that draws the blood from Christ's side is male; it is the original spear of wounding, the divine act of initiative out of which the world sprung, as it is also the spear of truth and healing which sheds the blood of total sacrifice.

The actual form of the chalice underwent many modifications. Originally made of a variety of materials, gold and silver were eventually decreed in the 9th century, with the exception of pewter for poorer communities. The original two handles died out during the 10th-12th centuries, and the hemispherical bowl only gave way in the 14th century to a more conical form. Many examples of chalices of these times are preserved due to the custom of ecclestiastics having the chalice and paten (q.v.) they had received at their ordination buried with them. From the 14th to the 16th centuries the stem is long, there is a pronounced baluster or 'knop', and the base is hexagonal in shape.

In the middle of the 16th century when elaboration in ornamentation was giving way to excess, came the Reformation, and the 'Communion Cup' replaced the chalice in Britain. There was much converting to the new form which resembled more a domestic beaker, larger, and allowing the laity to participate. The spirit of simplicity and a people's religion thus found its way into the sacrament, the focal point of meaning in the Church. (See 'sacrament'.)

1529

Chalice

1570

Communion Cup

CHANCEL

Latin *cancelli*, 'cross-bars' and *cancellare*, 'to enclose by a lattice'. Thus the meaning of the east end of a church containing the choir, clergy and altar, that is, the sacred area separated from the nave by a lattice called a 'chancel screen'. The screen is also known as the 'choir screen', 'pulpitum', or in a parish church 'rood-screen'. The chancel itself is also called the 'choir' and because there are daily choral services performed in the cathedral it is in this sense more applicable here, though the meaning behind the word 'chancel' is thereby lost. 'Sanctuary' and 'presbyter' are also loosely used for the sacred area east of the screen. All these terms are best considered together.

The underlying idea in the chancel is that of cancelling out by enclosure, of the protecting or screening of the holy secrets from profanation by the uninitiated masses, an aim found in all ancient religions and mystery rites. It existed in the inner sanctuary of the Jewish temple and in the early Christian church as a low wall and columns supporting a beam: both these were places for the guarding and dispensing of sacred mysteries, only due to those beings adequately prepared.

The Eastern Church has retained the emphasis on the mystery of the Mass by not celebrating it in open view, but behind the screen at the entrance to the sanctuary. In the West, such a separation of nave and chancel held until the time of the Reformation when the chancel was opened for the receiving of Communion by the congregation. This entailed destruction of most of the parish church 'rood-screens' and also of the stone images in the cathedral choir screen.

(Note the current imagery of the expression 'to cancel out' by the use of two cross-wise strokes.)

CHANCEL ARCH

The single stone arch at the entrance to the chancel found in the earliest Norman churches and common to all later parish churches in this country. It corresponds in form to the windows, so revealing the age of the church, and often bears signs of the later super-imposition of the rood-screen (q.v.).

CHANTRY or CHANTRY CHAPEL

French *chanteur*, Latin *cantare*, 'to sing'. A chantry is the name given to a chapel or altar or any part of a church where priests chanted prayers on behalf of the respected dead, as for instance the founder of that particular establishment, and later the landed families and their descendants connected with a parish. Their original function was to mitigate by prayer the suffering of the soul in purgatory. In this respect a chantry was often a bequest to provide such a privilege for the deceased.

Much importance was attached to the quality and magnificence of the craftsmanship in the stone screens, canopied niches and so on, in such chantries. In cathedrals an abbot, bishop or king would vie to produce the finest work, thus giving rise to many chantry chapels in one building. Equally, in the parish churches the families who were at the same time donors had their tombs built by the finest available craftsmen.

CHAPTER HOUSE

Old French *chapitre* (variant of *chapitle*), Latin *capitulum*, 'head of a column', which in turn is a diminutive of *caput*, 'head'. Thus a chapter is the head or governing body of a cathedral or collegiate church, meeting in the chapter house, a room or building attached to a cathedral for this purpose.

The chapter houses of English cathedrals are mainly polygonal with canopied stalls or a stone bench around the walls and a single column supporting the vault.

CHARGE

Old English, from Old French *chargier*, 'to put a load on'. Thus a connected meaning in heraldry of a figure carried on a shield – a 'bearing'. The object on the field, basic charges, are bands and linear motifs called 'ordinaires'. From the beginning, the horizontal bar had interchangeable names (i.e. 'fesse', 'barre', 'baston'), but the name quickly assumed more specific meanings. Crosses became variegated and fields subdivided, giving a complex vocabulary.

CHASUBLE

Medieval Latin *casubula*, diminutive of *casa*, 'cottage' – thus 'little cottage'. The chasuble is the embroidered and bejewelled covering over a priest's alb or cloak, suggesting a small shelter. Originally tent-like, with a hole for the head, the shape was modified to oval in accordance with Gothic idiom. Front and back have ordinary or Y-shaped crosses. During the celebration of the Eucharist, it is a reminder of the seamless garment of Christ, which signifies the unified power of the spirit. The Y symbolises the directing of spiritual force to the heart in priest and participant.

CHEST

Old English, from Latin *cista*, Greek *kistē*, 'basket'. Many kinds of old chest are found within the church. Some of the earliest remaining, originally referred to as 'trunks' because they were hollowed out trunks of trees, belong to the time of the Crusaders. These stem from the order of Henry II that parish churches should collect offerings towards the relief of the Holy Land: they have slits in the lid.

There were alms-boxes or poor-boxes which continued throughout the centuries, though the earliest were simply hollowed out, vertically standing trunks with lids. Also the church had need of chests for books and vestments and these are partitioned accordingly. Most of the early chests were banded with iron. It was only in the 13th century that chests began to be made from five planks with a sixth as a lid.

CHEVET

Old French *chevez*, from Latin *caput*, 'head'. A term used to describe the rounded apse when surrounded by an ambulatory (q.v.) with chapels. It is really a French feature but is found in some cathedrals as at Norwich, Gloucester and Westminster Abbey.

CHEVRON

Old French *chevron*, 'rafter'. The shape of the chevron is of an inverted letter V resembling a pair of rafters. It is used heraldically, and as a Norman moulding, where it is known as a 'zig-zag'.

CHIMNEY

Old French *cheminée*, Latin *caminus*, 'hearth', Greek *kaminos*, 'oven'. This is connected with *kamara*, 'vault'. The chimney was originally the whole structure – the fireplace and flue and projection above the building to take the smoke away. The chimneys in monastic buildings were hollowed out, vault-like spaces in the walls.

CHI-RHO MONOGRAM

(See under 'Monogram'.)

CHOIR or QUIRE

Greek *khoros*, 'dancing in a ring, a festive dance performed in a circle to the honour of the gods'. The choir in a church is the area east of the rood-screen ('chancel-screen' or 'choir screen' in a cathedral) between nave and sanctuary, which houses the choir or body of singers. It is often called the 'chancel'.

As the word indicates, Greek religious dances accompanied by singing were circular, reflecting the rotating solar system and vaster rotating systems in the universe of which man is a part. In the Greek theatre singing and dancing took place in the area below the stage, and this was called the *orkhēstra*, from *orkheisthai*, 'to dance' – whence the English 'orchestra'. Early Christian mystery rites had chanting to circular dances, but as Christianity became externalised, dance and music separated; the term 'choir' lost the implication of the dance, as later in the West the music assumed its independent role in the orchestra.

In the church, the function of the choir remained 'to honour God'. The monks who sang, men of a high spiritual order, mediated in their music between man and God. Enclosed by high partitions, within which latterly were the stalls with their beautiful canopies and misericords, they provided a centre of devotion. Here visual beauty and perfection of sound were conjoined in the act of worship. There is too the idea of the protection of something sacred or secret behind the screen, (see 'chancel'). Such secrets lie in music itself, for not only do the simplest musical ratios give the most perfect sounds, and every sound has its own unique power, but the early naming of notes themselves show that music was used to contain and disguise a cosmic hierarchy and the role of man's spiritual work within it. The monk-musician Guido d'Arrezo, as early as the 10th century, had named the currently used hexachord – UT, RE, MI, FA, SOL, LA. These letters are the first in the words of a Latin prayer, but there is an inner meaning. UT signifies the divine power in man, beyond all and beyond definition; this rises progressively through RE, Regina de Coeli, Queen of the Heaven, the moon, deadest of all matter – MI, Microcosmos, the earth and Man, the Divine image on that earth – FA, Fata, fate, the hold of the planetary forces over man's will – SOL, the sun whose warmth and light are life itself – LA, Lactea, the Milky Way, the galaxy to which man belongs.

LA
SOL
[*FA*
  MI
RE
UT

The overlapping of the hexachord was so arranged that the position of the semitone always fell between MI and FA. This position told that man's work was to overcome the inertias of the cosmic forces and to re-find his own will at the sun level, so that he might be of service in that hierarchy. Thus the use of the semi-tone in music was of great import: in fact the tri-tone, the interval of three whole tones by which the semi-tone was jumped, was given the name 'diabolus' (devil) and avoided accordingly. Without effort at that point, planetary forces were seen as working against man – thus the dictum of the time, 'Mi contra fa, Diabolus in musica'. The system was the basis of the later Tonic-Sol-Fa system and of the final complete major scale. (Mathematical proportion in music is discussed under 'organ', and the whole subject is treated in detail in the author's book 'The Hidden Face of Music'.)*

In some English cathedrals, where the eastern limb is short, the ideal form has been modified, the choir being pushed back through the transepts and covering the crossing. This holds, for instance, at Peterborough, Gloucester, and Westminster.

CHRISOM

Greek roots: *khrio*, 'anoint with oil' and *soma*, 'body'. Prior to 1552, baptism entailed a three-fold dipping of the child, who was then dressed by the priest in a white vesture called a chrisom. This was to be delivered back to the priest at the 'churching' of the mother (the ceremony of purification about a month after the birth). The chrisom was intended to symbolise the annointed or en-Christed body. In some effigies in churches, it is clear from the baptismal robe that the child has died within a month after birth.

CHRIST

Greek *khristos*, 'anointed one', *krisma*, 'an unguent'. Similarly, Messiah, our form of the Hebrew *mashiah*, literally means 'anointed one'.

To understand the signifance of Christ, we have to look at the ritual of anointing. From the beginning of history, oil has been used in the consecration of kings, places and temples. In the consecration of kings, oil poured over the head effected a transference of the power of the deity in whose name the rite was being performed. What then is the nature of oil? Oil

* Gollancz 1974

in the body allows the smooth functioning of the bones and sinew, as it does the parts of a machine; taken inwardly or used outwardly it is a lubricator and has powers of healing. Now the psychic counterpart of oil is love – it is man's egotism, his hate, which destroys his relationship with other men and creates a bitter chemistry in his body. Christ's message was one of love in that what he taught was to do with sacrificing the self-will to a Higher Will, and these forces of love give a fragrant oil and a flow of health in the body.

Words we may associate with 'Christ' are 'crux' and 'crucial', both of which have an implication of a 'crisis'. Greek *krisis* means 'a separation, a decision'. The decision is to do with the self-will, the point at which the bitter selfishness releases its hold and the healing oil operates – the same crisis as in the gold in a crucible or in the direction of an illness. The work of man, then, is to find the Christ in himself, a Christ who is being born whenever the oil of love begins to function. This brings the light of wisdom, for the other quality of oil is that it burns and gives light.

The English word oil is from Latin *oleum*, from Greek *elaion*, 'olive tree', an emblem of divine reconciliation and good will, whilst in Greece a crown of olive was the highest national distinction. Greek *kharis*, 'favour, grace', related to *khrisma*, is found in *eucharist*, thus *eu* 'good' with *kharis*, 'good grace': the Eucharist carries the essential idea of divine reconciliation, a re-membering of the individual soul into the Body of Christ through love.

Christ is the ultimate in sacrifice of self-will, but the en-Christing or anointing takes place in any being who is effecting this reconciliation between human and divine through his own sacrifice. Seen thus, Christ and oil are synonymous.

'Jesus' is a translation of the Hebrew word *Jehoshea*, 'Jah saves', that is, 'God saves'. 'Jesuah' and 'Joshua' are from the same source and the idea of liberator is in Joshua too, for this Old Testament forerunner led the children of Israel into the Promised Land. Thus the combined idea of a human being destined to save mankind as the vehicle of God himself, through the realising of his own anointing, his own inner rulership by love. As a pure instrument, it was the love of God that could be transmitted to man and the earth at that crucial moment in their evolution. Such a purity of being is suggested in the name 'Jesus', for the Hebrew *Jesse* means 'God exists' or 'God is'; Jesse is father to David and represents the

line from which Jesus was descended. (See 'Jesse Tree'.)
Later, Latin has this meaning in *esse*, 'to be'.

CHURCH

Stone circle

Knights Templar
Church, London

Anglo-Saxon *circe*, Western Germanic *kirike*, Greek
kuriakon, 'church': derived from Greek *kurios*, 'Lord,
master'. Thus the meaning of the Church as 'belonging to the
Lord'.

But there is also reference in the circe or kirk to the circle,
for properly the Church, the Body of God, is the whole of
nature, the universe in which one system revolves within
another. All belongs to the Lord – all is holy. The earth moves
within such a rotating cosmos, and from it the sun appears to
progress through the circular band known as the zodiac.
Standing stones of the Druids were circular in design, as were
temples and Christian rotundas – in fact the Holy Sepulchre
itself at Jerusalem, a Constantinian building, was round, and
the Knights Templars built most of their churches in that
form. Early sacred dances representing man's progression
through and subjection to these cosmic energies were also
circular. And the subtle chakras central to the teaching of
yoga are often represented as rotating discs of light.

The idea inherent in the kirk or circe is that in the creative
act the power of the Lord is locked in such systems, as it is in
the Church itself, a fact indicated sonically by the letter 'k' at
both ends of the word. For man, locked in such a system, with
its laws imposing upon him, the key to freedom lies symbolically in the non-rotating centre of the circle – the hub of the
wheel. Christ in this imagery is the thirteenth point at the
centre of the circle of twelve disciples, as Arthur is at the
Round Table of Knights. Only at the centre is the stillness of
the spirit. Equally, that stillness has to be found within the
closed system of the Church or it remains a dead form.

The English word 'church' however covers both *kuriakon*
and *ekklēsia*, and it is the latter that describes more clearly
the structure of the Church as a body of people. To the Greek
in pre-Christian times, *ekklēsia* meant 'an assembly of civil-
ians', really 'those called or summoned out' – (*ek*, 'out' and
kaleo, 'summon'). The original twelve disciples were the
prototypes of all those to be summoned out by Christ to a
life of sacrifice, a sacrifice which Christ affirmed by his volun-
tary death on a cross.

It was this ancient glyph of the cross which Christianity
eventually took over – though it was not until the 5th century

44

that it came to symbolise Christ's death on the cross. The cross, essentially a pinning to a point due to the intersection of two forces, represents sacrifice, of eternity to time, spirit to matter, or God to a mortal frame, and above all, for man, a universal to an individual consciousness. Christ's ritual enactment affirmed the image of sacrifice to the world, the need to sacrifice those temporal and material values brought about by the individual consciousness, by the ego. If these values are seen as the horizontal bar of the cross, the point at which they cross the eternal values should be one of balance, of release, where self (the bound personality) and Self (the eternal spirit) are seen to be aspects of each other. The death on the cross also pointed to the fact that each being was his own cross, that his 'I' consciousness could now effect his own release – something new in the evolution of man. This is the reason for the cross being the focus of Christianity, and also later the design of the church itself. (See 'cross' for a fuller account of this symbolism.)

Seen as an organisation, the first gathering of the twelve disciples was in effect the first Body of the Church. When the gift of tongues was made available at Pentecost the Church was alive by virtue of the Holy Spirit, and it was then a question of succession of authority. Early Christians held their gatherings in the houses of converts, but soon there was a need to adapt larger buildings: it was the adapted Roman basilica-type building that was called a *kuriakon*. The Eastern Orthodox Church retained the basilican plan whilst the Western Church moved to its own particular form, that of the Latin cross.

Looking at the purely physical resemblance between a man and the church, it could be said that man is his own church. With his feet touching the ground, vulnerable to the sensual level (the 'heel' in mythology), he can move up from the first moment of stimulation by the Holy Spirit (font) to a complete change of heart at the crossing, to a throat voicing new sounds of worship (the choir) and finally to an ultimate illumination in the head (the altar). This is inner spiritual ascent. (See 'cross', 'right and left', 'baptism', 'east end', 'west end', 'nave', 'Crucifixion'.)

CIBORIUM

A Latin word meaning 'drinking cup' from Greek *kiborion*, the 'fruit of the Egyptian water-lily' or 'a cup made in the form of that fruit'. The term has come to mean the vessel with a lid used for preserving the sacrament (the wafer or piece of bread given to the congregation at the Eucharist as a symbol of the Body of Christ). Originally, in the early church, such a vessel was suspended within a curtained canopy on four columns over an altar, but from the 13th century onwards the canopy fell into disuse and the vessel with a lid, standing on the altar, took its place. It is an interesting point that the chalice (the container of the wine at the Eucharist) also derives from the form of a flower. (See 'chalice'.)

CINQUEFOIL

French, literally 'five-leaves'. A figure of five equal curved sections often used to form a window, especially as an image of the five-petalled rose with its association with the Virgin Mary. (See 'rose'.)

CISTERCIAN

A monastic order formed in 1098 at Citeaux or Cistercium in Burgundy, a branch of the Benedictines. Because of their later connection with St. Bernard, who was regarded as a second founder, Cistercians in France and Germany were often called Bernadines. They were called 'white monks' because of the white frock over which, when outside the monastery, a black cloak was worn. Their monasteries following a pattern of austerity were built on lonely sites away from towns, as Tintern Abbey and the group in Yorkshire, Rievaulx, Byland, and Fountains.

CLERESTORY or CLEARSTORY

Literally 'clear-storey', from French *clair*, 'light' and storey, denoting the upper row of windows in the nave which is above the roof of the aisles, and so named because it allows in the light, whereas the triforium below it is a blind storey blocking out the light. Clerestories are only found in larger churches and cathedrals. (See 'bay'.)

CLERIC

Latin *clericus*, Greek *ḵlēriḵos*, 'belonging to the clergy'. *Kleros* in Greek means 'inheritance', and the idea among the early Christians was that the Christ power was passed down through those in authority. The 'cleric' or 'clerk' of the medieval times already indicated that writing and learning was vested in the Church. 'Clergy' is an old French modification of this – *clergie*, 'learning'.

CLOISTER

Latin *claustrum*, 'lock'; an 'enclosed place'. Thus in a monastic building it is a covered way that has the function of enclosing: usually it has a vaulted roof supported by pillars and is built south of the nave and west of the transept – the most sheltered area and one which catches the sun. The way looks in on all its sides onto a grassy enclosure (the cloister-garth) and the whole area served as a general meeting place of the monks.

The covered way gradually became more covered, was divided, and made into small studies (carrels) which were used by monks for writing and copying. Traces of these divisions can often be found.

CLUNIACS

The Cluniac monastic order was founded in 910 and took its name from its original house at Cluny in Burgundy, France. It was a reforming group advocating that the ecclesiastical authorities rather than kings should have the power to appoint members of the clergy. None of the greatest English monasteries were of this order, though a feature of their architectural design, the double transept, was adopted in many cathedrals. At the time of the Suppression there were twenty houses in Britain.

COCK

Old Englsh *coce*, Low Latin *coccus*, connected with Low Latin *coccum*, 'scarlet berry', after the colour of the comb. The comb is serrated and bears the idea of division, and through its blood-red colour, of sacrifice. The crowing of the cock heralds the day and to the Greeks, the cock was dedicated to Apollo through association with the rising sun of intelligence, and to Aeschylus through health from early rising and early bed-going. But the day is the day of the natural world, of light, which in one sense is an adversary of the spirit (see 'Lucifer'). Thus in announcing the day, there is pride: the cock crows on his own dunghill.

The idea of Peter's denial of Christ belongs here: human beings weep bitterly when they realise their error of pride and its consequence, the fall into a material world. Thus the cock on the weather-vane of the church is a constant reminder of the danger of the denial of the spirit: a coxcomb is a fool in the worldly sense. It suggests here and elsewhere in Christian

47

symbolism the need for watchfulness. In Eastern mythology the cock symbolises lust and pride. Thus there are two faces to the cock – one the waking state and the other death, to the evolving spirit.

COCKATRICE

Old French *cocatrice*, 'ichneumon', Latin *coctrice* from *calcatric*, 'the tracker'. The Latin *calcare* means 'to track', a description from the Greek of the *ikhneumon*, a small animal that breaks the eggs of crocodiles to destroy them.

The French cocatrice became one of the many medieval mythological beasts, said to be hatched out of a cock's egg by a reptile. Its glance was said to be able to kill. In heraldry, the head, wings and legs were those of a cock, and its body and tail those of a serpent.

The cocatrice also has the name 'basilisk' and is found on finials and outer walls of cathedrals.

COLOUR

Latin *color*, 'colour' – in general – and 'outward appearance' connected with Latin *celare*, 'to hide, keep secret'. Other connections all suggest 'concealing'. Colour in the sense indicated in the word is a disguise on a primary unified light or truth: it is a differentiation which destroys unity, as number begets numbness. Both are part of the *maya* (illusion) of creation.

In Church symbolism, altar coverings, hangings in general, and the chasubles of the priests, change according to the particular festival. In iconography and in more general symbolism, the use of colour is based on a primary triad which corresponds in essence with three aspects of power, the nature of the three Persons of the Trinity.

The Father, the energy source of Will, is red (hot); the Son, formative idea world or Word, ordering and limiting that energy, is blue (cold); and the Holy Spirit, mediating force, the flow of life itself, is yellow (neither hot nor cold). On a human level this is reflected in many contexts, but it remains basically the red of action, the blue of thought and the yellow of mediation and of healing. Each colour has a positive and negative aspect, the divine, as against the fallen, man. Red is pure will, but negatively rage, 'seeing red': blue is perfect logical clarity, but negatively a 'blue funk', the interference of the dualistic mind: yellow is pure love but negatively self-interest, 'he's yellow', the yellow of cowardice and lack of courage. (Thus the colour of the garments worn by Judas.)

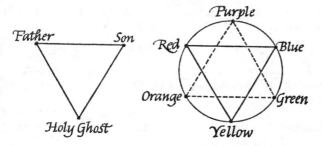

Red then is always energy, a creative or destructive energy. Blue is the colour of the Son, but since the world is conceived not only in mind but also through matter, the womb of matter, the Virgin Mary, is also given the colour blue: it is light and clear indicating the purity of her Wisdom. Yellow is the colour of gold, the untarnishable spirit and indicates the luminous radiance of the divine state.

Secondary colours, those resulting from the admixture of two primary colours, are to do with the relationship of man to God – his striving. Each has to be seen in relation to the colours of which it is composed and also in relation to its opposite primary colour. (See the diagram.) Green is a colour of development, orange of fruitful love, and purple is the colour of man's possible kingship, his own Self authority. Negatively, if there is no will, no striving to the divine state, green is stunted growth (green with envy, sickly green), orange is false love and purple is mortality as opposed to eternity.

In the Church, purple is associated with the man Jesus Christ, King, a state reached only through sacrifice; thus it also symbolises mourning, penitence, and renunciation. Red, the colour of energy, also refers to the blood of sacrifice, as in the blood of martyrs, and to the very first sacrifice, that of the Father in begetting the world. Gold or yellow, because of its associations with the fire of the Holy Spirit, is connected with festivals, as more commonly, is white. White (Christmas, Easter, Ascension) is used to denote rejoicing, because it embraces the whole spectrum of colour in one, thus representing the undifferentiated spirit: and in the same way, black is connected with deprivation and mourning.

The use of colour in the Church is however not accurately predictable. A general rule layed down at the beginning of the 13th century suggested white for feasts, red for martyrs, black for penitential seasons, and green for others; this remained unclarified until a rubric of greater complexity was laid down in 1570.

COLUMN

Latin *columna*, 'pillar'; related to Latin *columen*, 'height, summit'. A column is a pillar of stone carrying the weight of a superstructure.

In ancient Greece there were three main types or orders of column, deriving from certain areas and periods, notably Doric, Ionic, and Corinthian. The quality of each column found expression in its total shape and proportion, especially in its capital (q.v.). The transition from one to another historically is an expression of the unfolding of the three-fold structure of the human being.

The Doric column (q.v.) was formed in the masculine image, inspired by the gymnasts of Olympia – it stood for controlled balance, and power of the will. The Ionic column (q.v.) was formed in the elegant feminine image, on the poetry and grace of the artist and the material concepts of the Ionic philosophers. The Corinthian (q.v.) column was modelled on the sharper edges of the Attic philosophy of Plato and Aristotle. Its acanthus leaf represented the flowering of the intellect. This three-fold development is indicated in the balanced format of the three-storey building: the Doric is the lowest order, the Ionian the middle, and the Corinthian the highest. It is also an inherent division in the human being which follows the nature of the Trinity of forces in all religions – will, feeling, thinking. In this way the human body is divided, into energies and appetites, heart, and head, as the individual limbs are similarly constituted – viz. upper arm, forearm and hand. The column itself is three-fold, consisting of base, shaft, and capital, as the entablature (q.v.) is also composed of three parts. (Compare each order and refer to 'pillar' for further symbolism.)

COMMUNION RAIL

Due to the spirit of the Reformation there was much disorder in the state of the churches from the mid-16th century. There was, for example, the controversy over the position of the altar or communion table: the Eucharist was seen either as belonging to the body of the church or as a sacred sacrifice belonging to the chancel end. Prior to the Reformation, 'houseling benches' (q.v.), movable benches, were used for communicants, but Archbishop Laud finally decided the issue during his primacy (1633-41), placing the table at the east end and introducing communion rails, stipulated to be about a yard high. At the same time, among other things, he introduced the Italian credentia or credence table (q.v.).

CONSECRATION CROSS

Latin *consecrare*, 'to dedicate, consecrate' (*con* and *sacer*, 'holy'). From the 12th century onwards, when churches were consecrated, the walls were anointed with oil and marked with a cross. Customarily there were three crosses for each wall, inside and outside, making twenty-four in all. Traces of these crosses, of varied design, are still to be found.

COPE

Allied to 'cape', from Medieval Latin *capa*, and originally from Latin *caput*, 'head'. Thus, 'a covering for the head'. Now the word denotes a long cloak worn by clergy on ceremonial occasions.

CORBEL

French *corbel* or *corveau*, Latin *corvus*, 'raven'. A corbel is a block of stone projecting from a wall, suggestive of the projecting beak of the raven. It serves as a support, taking internal structures such as beam or vaulting, and is often beautifully carved. When there are a large number of such corbels in a line below the roof eaves (there are some remarkable examples in Norman churches), such a group is called a 'corbel table'.

CORINTHIAN (COLUMN)

From Corinth, a part of ancient Greece having its own style of architecture, the other two being Doric and Ionian; graceful in proportions as the Ionic column, with fluted shaft and a capital of carved acanthus leaves. It is said that the architect Cellemachus had a vision of the acanthus motif hanging over the grove of a virgin – a symbolic image of the takeover of the female Ionic phase in Greek history by the phase of the faculty of reason. The scroll form of the acanthus leaf is used in Roman work and continues wherever the classical influence is found. The order is the highest in a three-storey building.

CORNICE

Italian *corona*, 'crown, cornice': a horizontal projecting moulding directly under the eaves of a roof, and carved according to the style of the period.

CREDENCE or CREDENCE TABLE

Medieval Latin *credentia*, Latin *credere*, 'to believe, trust'. The small table by the side of the altar on which the bread and wine are placed ready for the Eucharist. The term is a reference to the commital of faith in the act of celebrating the mass. Laud introduced the credence at the beginning of the 17th century.

CRESSET STONE

Old French *craisse*, 'grease', Latin *crassus*, 'thick'. From grease comes the meaning of a vessel for holding burning oil or pitch. A cresset stone is a block of stone with one or more cup-shaped holes, used for containing oil or candles for use in lighting churches in medieval times.

CREST

Old French *creste*, Latin *crista*, 'a cock's comb or tuft on the head of animals'. Thus, a tuft, originally worn on helmets as distinctive identification in battle when the arms on a shield would be lost to sight. In heraldry, a crest is a personal device depicted above the shield.

CROCKETS

A variant of *crochet* which is a diminutive of *croche* or *croc*, a Germanic word meaning 'hook'. Like the musical note, the crotchet, the Gothic architectural device of the same name, is in the form of a hook. Carved projecting hooks decorate the spires, pinnacles and canopies, either stone or wood, of our churches and cathedrals. The varieties of form are innumerable and correspond to the particular period of architecture.

CROSS

The word 'cross' replaced the Old English word *rod*. All forms of the word come from Latin *crux* (genitive *crucis*), 'cross', and this is from an Aryan base *ker*, 'to grow', from which the word 'create' derives.

The symbol of the cross is as old as the history of man. It is an image of one force intersecting another, and is essentially to do with the duality resultant upon creation. Thus there are many possible interpretations. The horizontal line can be seen as the substantial world, female, and the vertical line as the initiating force of spirit, male – both aspects of each other and of God himself: thus on the physical plane it can be taken as a sexual symbol. Or the cross can be seen as time (horizontal line) with eternity (vertical line) cutting through it at any and all points: again both are aspects of each other. The presence of such a duality makes for man's frustrations: he is aware of the conflict in the levels of his being – thus the state of mind 'cross', meaning angry. But the fact that there is a point at which the two coincide and become one, redeems all, for in it duality may disappear. The secret of the cross lies in the fact that one arm, the horizontal time one, is gravely out of balance with the eternal. The dying on the cross is the sacrifice of error and sin (sin is best translated from Greek as 'what has missed the mark'), so that both are equally balanced, and so that at the point of pinning, eternity and time, spirit and matter, may be seen as non-dual. Thus the eastern concept of immediacy and a here-and-now awareness – the realisation of eternity in the middle of time; also the importance of the 'crossing' or 'transept' in the church.

Eternity

Time

Historically a cross in a circle antedates one out of a circle – to abstract it denotes a stage in man's evolution, when he has been removed out of an embracing spiritual whole into physical separation. One of the earliest crosses taken out of the circle was the Egyptian T or Tau cross where the horizontal line is seen simply as a bar imposing a limit upon the extent of the vertical line, for, as has been said elsewhere, creation means a restriction on power. In the other Egyptian cross, the 'crux ansata', the handled cross or '*ankh*', the cross of time is taken out of the circle of eternity which remains above it as the guiding supra-human power. As with the western cross, which can be seen as a tree of death or of life, it is two-faced, for though it is a cross of limitation, it is also the holy cross of Life borne by Thoth. It also resembles the glyph of Venus, whose attributes, though to do with the higher aspects of love, are also to do with the lower ones of physical generation.

Tau

Ankh

Venus

Even the circle is open to a dual interpretation, for though because of its unceasingness it is a symbol of eternity, it is also

53

a ring of limitation holding what is inside it captive. (See 'church'.) In this sense it represents the limiting power of all the repetitive cycles of nature and time – thus man is fixed in that circle upon his own particular cross. This gives the other face of the cross in the circle, the individuated point within the manifest universe, at the centre of the four points of the compass, the four fixed signs of the zodiac (see 'Evangelists'), the eastern mandala, and other archetypal images denoting the establishing of power. The function of the cross is to fix onto a point, and in fact, the number 4, whichever glyph we take, is essentially a cross and denotes the physical plane of existence.

Despite this ancient symbolism, early symbols such as the fish, the lamb, and the lion, were initially used to represent Christ; it was only in the 5th century that the cross was used to express the central meaning of Christianity. This cross was of two kinds – the Greek cross geometrically perfect, and the Latin cross, formally suited to take the transfixed body of Christ. It was the latter that was adopted later as the plan for the church building.

It is more likely, however, that the cross upon which Christ died was a simple stake or T cross. Moreover, such a stake is symbolically the sacrificial tree, the tree of many mythologies that represents the created world, the proliferation of life and the sacrifice by God of his own power. In Scandinavian mythology and in the Kabala the roots of the tree arise in heaven,

Rood   Altar

54

a clear image of this truth. It is the tree upon which all men are nailed, and yet it is also the Tree of Life. Here is the dual aspect of the cross again.

We find the same truth in the placing of the crosses in the church building. First, before the chancel at the place of the crossing is the tree or cross upon which Christ was crucified – the cross of suffering and death: this is the traditional rood (q.v.) upon the rood-beam which was a key feature of all parish churches up to the time of the Reformation. More generally in the crucifix, finity and duality are shown in a variety of ways: the sun and moon are shown to the right and left respectively of Christ, the Dove is above and the skull below his body, and the thieves at either side are those of time, past and future, the dual process of thought which robs a man of immediate awareness. The other cross or tree is that of Life, properly found on the altar: in this cross, Christ, and potentially the Christ in all men, reigns in glory with the aureole of illumination – it is the result of the sacrifice and renunciation on the first cross, the state of Christus Rex where all is seen as One, and a man is a mere vehicle for the awakened God in him (see 'Ascension'). Today a plain cross is generally seen on the altar, a partial loss of meaning, but where there is a crucifix of the first sort, this is a misunderstanding of the symbolism.

Many types of cross are seen in iconography, most of which stem from heraldry. Surmounting a staff, and carried before them in procession a triple bar signifies a Pope, a double cross signifies an archbishop, and a single cross a bishop (see diagram). A cross elevated on three steps is called a Calvary cross, the steps symbolising the three graces, Faith, Hope and Charity. The cross with its ends in the form of a fleur-de-lis, is called a cross-fleury. The cross with four small ones within its arms is the Jerusalem cross, the five crosses in all symbolising the five wounds of Christ. (It was the insignia, established by the Crusaders, of Jerusalem.) (See 'Maltese cross', 'pattée 'cross', 'raguly cross', 'St. Andrew's cross' or 'cross decussata', and 'Tau' or 'St. Anthony's cross'.)

CROSSING

The name given to the area between the transepts and before the chancel or rood screen (pulpitum in a cathedral). Above is the central tower or lantern which allows light to fall onto this area. (For the symbolism of the crossing see 'cross', 'transepts', 'church', 'lantern', 'Ascension'.)

Crozier
head

Old French *crossier*, 'the one bearing the cross' in the early Church, though later the word came to mean the actual staff itself. The roots of 'crozier' are however Germanic, giving *crucche*, 'crutch or staff' in Middle English. The 'crook' of the shepherd from the same root has the image of drawing sheep into the fold, and reflects the pastoral function of the bishop.

The staff or wand of office, originally a simple wooden walking stick with a curved handle, and always a symbol of authority, was one of the most hallowed possessions of the early Christian saints, capable of transmitting magical powers. In Ireland especially, the staff was guarded zealously as a relic capable of effecting magical cures, and the metal shrines made as protection were of great artistic merit. In England the staff was blessed in the consecration of a bishop as early as the 9th century, and its power is also seen in the legend of the staff of Joseph of Arimathea which bore the Christmas-flowering hawthorn.

Representations of the pastoral staff are seen frequently in monumental effigies in churches, but most of the actual staves (it is the heads of these staves which in the Middle Ages became the vehicle for much beautiful ivory work) were destroyed at the Reformation. It was always held in the left hand so as to allow the right to be free for ritual acts such as blessing.

The symbolism of the 'rod' or 'staff' is connected with the Tree of Life, the vertical force of growth and aspiration whether in nature or in man. In man this force is located around the spinal column where it may rise in the form of transmuted sex energy: whether it is seen in the Greek '*caduceus*' or in the snake of Yogic Kundalini, the staff of authority has been realised when the power from the earth or sex level has been regenerated to become the flower in the head.

CRUSADER

With many European versions of the word, from *cruciata* (past participle of *cruciare*, 'to mark with a cross'), denoting the cross worn by those fighting for the cause of Christ.

The object of the crusaders was the recovering of the Holy Land from the Saracen invaders. This was successfully accomplished in 1099 by a mainly French force, the first Crusade;

but Saladin the Sultan of the Saracens recaptured it in 1187. Later crusades were an attempt to regain the lost ground.

The Third Crusade (1189-93) is significant in Britain since it was led by Richard I (the Lionheart) and included knights from throughout Europe. The seven crusades occurred between the years 1096 and 1270.

The stone effigies of crusaders in churches often have the left leg bent at the knee. This is a mnemonic of the sacrifice of the self-will to the service of Christ, and reflects the image of Christ on the Cross. (See 'right and left'.)

CRUCIFIXION

Latin *crucifixus*, 'one fixed to a cross' (*crux*, 'cross' and *fixus*, past participle of *figere*, 'to fix'). The Crucifixion is the focal point in Church doctrine and iconography. It can be taken however on many levels – the fixing of time in eternity, the fixing of spirit within matter, the fixing or incarnating of God as man in the world, and on a psychological level in man, the conscious fixing and dying to the old self in the work of regeneration.

In Christ and in man, the freeing from the crucified state, from the mechanical world, is a *conscious* death or crucifixion. Such a sacrifice involves the surrender of the self-will to the Will of the Father, which in renderings of the Crucifixion is always symbolised by the fall of the head to the right (right heraldically – left as seen by the spectator). The right side is the side of Will, and the necessary death is of the forces invested in the left or devilish side, the side of the rational, egotistic man. For the same reason in iconography the left leg of Christ is pinned under the right leg which remains straight – though this occurs regularly only after the 13th century. The spear pierces Christ's right side, for the blood is the regenerated blood which is the healing force for man on earth.

Such a central theme contains much symbolism, and many images associated with the historical fact are found everywhere in sculpture, art and furnishings in churches. They include: the stigmata; the crown of thorns; the seamless garment; purple robe; ladder; rope and chain for the deposition of the body; the ewer used by Pilate to wash his hands; hammer and pincers; spear which lanced Christ's side, and chalice containing the blood; the pillar of scourging; two thieves.

Of these the stigmata represent the sacrifice of the sensual life (five senses, five wounds); the seamless garment represents the pure and undivided spirit; the two thieves at right and left represent the loss of unity through the duality inherent in time; the purple robe signifies royalty; the spear and chalice represent respectively the self-willed sacrificial death, male act of initiative, and the female container, the world (see 'chalice') which receives the redeeming effect of that shed blood; the sponge of vinegar on a reed symbolises the very bitterest dreg of suffering attendant upon total renunciation of self-will – the last thing to be tasted by Christ in this world. The reed here is a symbol of great antiquity in mystery rites – it is that power which bends but does not break, symbolising the authority of the Spirit in the sacrificial act.

In iconography there are two crucifixes – Christ suffering and Christ triumphant. (These are discussed under the heading 'cross'.) Historically it is only after the 11th century that Christ is shown naked and dead. Previously he was fully clothed with eyes open and with two feet nailed separately to the cross (see 'icon'). Significant symbolism, established in medieval times, gave way later to the degraded sentimentalism in which inner experience had become a formal shell.

CRYPT

Latin *crypta*, 'a vault', Greek *kruptos*, 'hidden'. The word denotes an underground chamber beneath a church used as a chapel or burial place. The crypt was especially hallowed in early Christianity since the bones of saints and founders were put there and became shrines which could only be viewed from an opening on ground level. (See 'tomb'.)

CUPOLA

Italian from Low Latin *cupa*, 'cup', Latin *cupola*, a diminutive of *cupa*, 'tub'. Thus, a roof resembling an inverted cup, the outside of which is usually a dome.

CURATE

Low Latin *curatus*, 'one who has the care of souls' (Latin *cura*, 'care'). The word 'cure' is also derived from this root, and thus a curate is a healer of souls. The incumbent or vicar of a parish originally had the name of 'curate', but now the title is reserved for an assistant.

CUSP

Latin *cuspis*, 'a point'. One of the points projecting from the underside of an arch, giving a trefoil or multifoil form to the arch. Cusps originated in the later part of the Early English style, when they sometimes terminated in a leaf.

D

DADO

Italian *dado*, 'cube, pedestal'. The pedestal (small column) between the base and the cornice. Architecturally it has come to mean the lower part of the walls in a room when decorated differently from the upper, especially by panelling with mouldings resembling a continuous pedestal. It is usually separated from the upper half by a moulding.

DAGGER MOTIF

A common motif in the window tracery of the Decorated style, pointed at the foot and either round or pointed at the head. The inside is cusped. When the motif is curved it is a 'mouchette'. It is common in the complex curves of the 'flamboyant style'. (See 'tracery'.)

DEACON and DEACONESS

Greek *diakonos*, 'a servant'. The most junior rank in the ordained ministry, below a priest and bishop.

DEAN

Latin *decanus* from *decem*, 'ten'. Originally a monk supervising ten novices, a dean is now a senior priest in charge of a cathedral, or, as a rural dean, a subsection of a diocese.

DECORATED PERIOD

A period of English architecture following on from Early English, from 1307-77, broadly equated with the 14th century. It is so called because the simplicity of the early style changes into ornateness. Decoration now predominates. Windows have geometric and flowery tracery (see 'tracery'), the clearstory is heightened, vaulting has many ribs giving an effect of star shapes, and the ogee arch is used. The names Geometric and Curvilinear used in relation to this period really refer to the tracery in the windows.

DENTIL

Latin *dens*, 'a tooth': thus a decorated classical motif on a moulding.

DEVIL

Middle English *devel*, Latin *diabolus*, Greek *diabolos*, 'slanderer' (Greek *diaballein* is 'to slander, accuse'). In art, the devil is illustrated with a tail, hair, horns and claws, indicating a close affinity with animality, a statement about the present stage in man's evolution. Though man began with divine powers, he became subject to the lower mind, to animal passions, to the prison of the senses, and to a consuming awareness of self. The divine did not die but lived at variance with this animality: thus a man's will may be directed in either of these directions. If it follows his ego and the sensual life, it may be summed up in the glyph of the pentacle showing the horns of the goat, or if it follows his spiritual Self, aiming at the control of the senses, it may be summed up in the truly balanced five-pointed star, a human being erect and balanced on the earth (see diagram p. 61).

But to label the devil as 'bad' is an error of rational thinking. Inner teaching says that the devilish forces, the world of the spirits that numbs the Spirit, are in fact the sounding board of development – the devil is merely God developing. Such

a connection is easily seen in the words 'devil' and 'develop'.
God in this sense is the goat, the original scapegoat – all can
be blamed on Him: and the material world is 'Deus Inversus',
God inverted. Unless this is understood, power locked in a
given physical form continues to be deficient: if a man locks
himself in his own separate existence he succumbs to the
'Devil' and lives in his own Hell. All he has to do is to
acknowledge the source.

Hell is represented as a region of chaos, of animality, of
aimless movement and the acrid fires of hate. This again is
the unredeemed world of the senses. A man can go deeper
into this living Hell unless its value as a whetting stone to
reach Heaven is acknowledged. 'Hell' is a singularly light
word for what it is supposed to denote, and 'Heaven' is a singularly heavy word, suggesting that it is not attained without
something first being 'heaved' up. Both are aspects of power
and can be related to the west and east ends of the church
(q.v.). Note the medieval carvings on fonts at the west end
showing the struggle against evil. Moreover, the word 'evil'
can be seen to belong to 'devil', or it can be seen as division in
the will (de-vil): as boustrophedon it reads 'live', showing
the two aspects of divine energy, and anagramatically it becomes a 'veil' upon true power. (See 'five wounds' and
'Satan'.)

DEXTERA DEI

Literally 'the right hand of God' but referred to simply as
'the hand of God': in iconography the image is of a hand,
usually issuing out of a cloud and representing God the Father
– the First Person of the Trinity. The symbol of the hand was
originally used because of the obvious difficulty of personify-
ing an abstract power. But about the 9th century God the
Father began to be represented as the middle figure of three
Persons, and by the 16th century, with God shown in pontifi-
cal robes, the externalised form has degraded the simple symbol.

The image of the hand was still used in medieval times and
is found in many Old Testament scenes, such as the sacrifice
of Isaac, Moses and the Burning Bush, Moses receiving the
Law, etc., and in many of the principal incidents of Christ's
life in the New Testament. It is used whenever God inter-
cedes on behalf of man, speaking to him or blessing him.
This intercedence is suggested in the hand reaching downwards and also in the open palm. The hand has, in fact, its

own three aspects corresponding to the aspects of the Trinity – the closed fist, the energy of which is as yet unleashed (Father), the fingers, capable of precise shaping of raw material (Son), and the palm of the hand, receptive and open in an attitude of love (Holy Spirit). The Dextera Dei expresses the love in the Father's power. (See 'blessing' and 'right and left'.)

DISCIPLES

Latin *discipulus*, 'a learner, pupil', related to *discere*, 'to learn'. The word disciple is closely connected with the disciplines presented by a teacher. In the New Testament there are twelve disciples, each representing one part of the whole, as a teacher represents the whole. Each is determined in his actions by a unique psychic pattern related to cosmic energies represented by the twelve signs of the zodiac. (The number 12 is significant as a multiple of 3 and 4: three aspects of absolute power, as in the Trinity, unmanifest, play through the four elements of the manifest world, giving twelve permutations. It is a number of developmental progression seen in the rose window of the cathedral.

Because each being has a unique energy pattern which he acts out to the exclusion of others, his main discipline is to become aware of these others, and to awaken them inside himself so as to become a whole man: this awakening opens the door to his own divinity. For this reason Christ is properly at the centre of a round table as was King Arthur. Christ and Arthur are the potentially whole man, and the beings around symbolise the differentiated types. Whenever the number 12 is seen in mythology, as in the twelve Labours of Hercules, and even in the twelve members of the modern jury, there is the

Water
Air
Earth
Fire

Mutable (Holy Spirit)
Fixed (Son)
Cardinal (Father)

Rose window

idea of seeking a whole by bringing together the fruits of the twelve's differentiated parts. In hearing and spreading the gospel in their unique ways, the disciples were continuing their fundamental symbolism. (See 'apostles' and 'Last Supper'.)

DOG-TOOTH

The most characteristic ornament on moulding in Early English architecture, known as dog-tooth because it consists of four leaf-forms drawn up to a point resembling the tooth of a dog.

DOMINICANS

One of the four main orders of friars (brothers depending upon alms for their existence) named after St. Dominic who founded the order in 1205 – they are sometimes known as the O.P. – Order of Preachers, and first came to this country in 1221, founding a house in Oxford. Due to their black mantle over a white habit they also became known as Black Friars.

DOOM

Old English *dom*, Old High German *tuom*, judgement, decree': from an Aryan root 'to do' or 'to put'. The 'doom' is the name given to a medieval painting or stage depiction of a scene where the damned are pitchforked by the devil into the mouth of hell – a version of the Last Judgement. It was often found in medieval churches in the form of a tympanum covering the area between the chancel arch and the rood screen.

The idea of judgement suggests that the voice of God Himself (compare Latin *dominus*, 'lord') has issued the decree, and thus the devil is here the other face of God, the ruthless judge. The original majestic aspect of the devil, however, gave way to a farcical aspect in which he became the butt of ridicule and the buffoon of the medieval stage. In this guise, all that was base in human nature could be expiated – and the devil became a scapegoat. The later Punch and Judy show is a continuation of the same theme, with Punch the devil being irreverently knocked on the head and ridiculed.

DORIC COLUMN

From *Doris*, one of the partitions of ancient Greece. It is the strongest and most ancient of columns, massive, without base, with a simple capital and shallow fluting. The diameter is approximately 2/11ths of the height. In a three-eyed building, where each storey has a different order, the Doric is always the lowest. The Doric column was formed on a strong masculine image, complementary with the Ionic column which was based on the elegant female form. The Romans, whilst keeping the proportions, introduced a plinth and scalloped flutings.

DORMITORY

Low Latin *dormitorium*, 'sleeping room', *dormire*, 'to sleep'. The sleeping room in a monastery sometimes abbreviated to DORTER.

DORTER

An abbreviation of 'dormitory', the sleeping room in a monastery (See above). The 'rere-dorter' (q.v.) is the room containing closets, behind the sleeping quarters.

DOVE

Middle English *dūve*, Gothic *dūbo*, related to Old English *dūfan*, 'to dive', from an Aryan base meaning 'to go down into water'. The dove is a symbol of the Holy Ghost, and as such is found carved on font covers, in representations of the baptism of Christ, the Annunciation to the Virgin Mary, and in the creation of the world. It is a symbol of the reconciliation between God and man, spirit and matter: it is the symbol of God's love for his creation.

In the New Testament, the Spirit of God is said to descend like a dove, and images show the bird diving head first out of heaven onto earth, from eternity into time, following the imagery inherent in the origin of the word. That descent of the spirit is a baptism by fire in the purified waters of the material world – that is into a material vehicle ready to receive it: a man has to be prepared before its power becomes available. As the nature of the dove is innocent and guileless, so a man is selfless and harmless when he is spiritually regenerated.

In a wider sense of cosmic evolution, the Holy Spirit constantly saves and reconciles, sowing seeds of new beginnings and rekindling the new out of what has been discarded: in this sense, the dove brought an olive branch into the ark of Noah, rescuing truth from the flood of error and indicating reconciliation between God and man. In another sense the Latin word for dove is *columba*, and Columbine in the origins of pantomime represents the human soul, female, selfless and the companion of Harlequin, the pure spirit. Thus she is the mediator between the spirit and the body, belonging to one and involved in the other. Strangely the column (Latin *columna*), so integral to the church building, is a support between ground and roof, again reflecting the function of mediation between high and low.

DRAGON

Greek *drakon*, 'a dragon, serpent'. It is literally to do with sight – Greek *derkomai*, 'to see'; thus 'one who sees'. The sight here suggested is that of the physical world and the attendant time-process. The chief enemy of man's spirit in his involvement in this world, the sight or the dragon, can be seen as a devourer of the free spirit. This is the same dialectic as is found in 'Lucifer' where the word means 'bringer of light' though he is in effect the 'Prince of Darkness'. Sight is a great gift, but it seeps away man's inner sight: the dragon may bring fire, but it burns up all in its path.

The killing of the dragon in Christian art represents the overcoming of forces that hold man in bondage. St. George who kills the dragon is literally 'earth worker', and equally St. Michael (Hebrew, 'he who is like unto God') is shown clad in his armour fighting the same fight of the spirit, as do all children of God. Satan is that force of evil epitomised and is shown in the guise of a serpent or dragon.

DRIPSTONE or WEATHER-MOULDING

A stone or projecting moulding which takes away the dripping of water from above a door or window, and is in some instances used decoratively on the inner wall of a building. (See 'hood-moulding'.)

DRUID

Old Celtic *druid* – *dru* and *wid*. *Dru* means 'very strong' and *wid*, 'to know': thus 'very wise'. *Wid* is the same root as *wit*, related to Latin *videre*, 'to see' and Old English *wis*, 'wise'. The *dru* part of the word is also related to Greek *drus*, 'oak' or 'tree'.

Druidism is an ancient Celtic system of religion, governed by a priesthood, a repository of learning covering all conceivable subjects within an embracing cosmology. The extant writings, dating from before the advent of Christianity, belie the notion that Britain was a savage place before the coming of the Romans. There are many remarkable similarities in the

65

early canons to the tenets of early Christianity, and it is little wonder that the Druidism of Wales was absorbed so readily into early Christian monasticism.

E

EAGLE

Low Latin *aquila*, 'eagle', Latin *aquilus*, 'dark-skinned', with reference to the colour of the bird. Classically a symbol of victory of higher over lower, as when it is represented with talons on a hare or a serpent, but this is only in the sense of order being superior to chaos. In Christianity the eagle came to represent the victory of the Logos or Word over that unformulated power, and thus over all enemies of the spirit.

With its gift of seeing all from a great height (air is a symbol of the intellect), the eagle is associated with this Higher Intellect of St. John, and in the church, the Word of God, the Bible, is read under the open wings of the carved eagle which graces the lectern (q.v.).

When depicted fighting with a serpent conflict is between the root power of God and His ordering intelligence – a conflict because intelligence is a limit to that power. It is, in fact, the Son opposing the Father, an opposition referred to in early Christianity. But the aim of the opposition is not the killing of the Father by the Son, the serpent by the eagle, but the return of the Son, the fulfilling of the Word and a reconciliation with the Father. This is seen in the story of the Prodigal Son and in the pattern of a man's life. Energy and intelligence then work harmoniously together, and the image becomes one of the eagle and serpent affectionately intertwined.

The two-headed eagle of the Eastern Church, looking right and left, affirms the power of the overseeing Logos over the dualities inherent in time and space. The eagle, as the constellation representing St. John and as one of the four creatures associated with the Evangelists, is explained under 'Evangelist'. (See 'lectern'.)

EARLY ENGLISH

The period of architecture following upon the Norman, beginning in 1189 and continuing until 1307; it is thus broadly equated with the 13th century. Notable features are – tall lancet windows and pinnacles, and groups of slender

shafts replacing solid Norman pillars: other features are buttresses, foliated capitals and graceful rib and panel vaults.

EAST END

'East' is from a Germanic root *austr*, 'east', which is connected with Latin *Aurora* and Greek *eos*, both meaning
'dawn'.

The orientation of the church with the altar at the east end
derives from ancient pagan traditions. Monuments, such as
Stonehenge, the Parthenon, and the temple at Luxor, have
entrances facing the rising sun, which was clearly regarded
as a divine life-giving power. When the form of the basilica
was adopted by the early Christians, there was some arbitrariness, but by the time of the monasteries and cathedrals, the
ancient orientation had been permanently reaffirmed.

The sun was symbolically seen as the Son, that is as Christ
the Son of God, since it was seen to resurrect daily and
annually out of darkness, as Christ rose from the darkness of
the tomb into eternal life. The power of resurrection in all its
forms, whether it is seen in the cosmos at Christmas and
Easter, or psychologically in the re-righting of man's fallen

Spirit
light
E
|
W
Dark
matter

67

energies, is a function of male will, of the spirit reaffirming power over matter, life over death. East is connected with Easter; Easter is from Eastre, the English goddess of Light and Spring whose festival was celebrated at the vernal equinox. Thus the lancet window symbolically belongs to the east end of a church (and where its three divisions are under one arch, the unity of the Trinity), whilst the rose window, as female, belongs to the west end. The entry into a church at the west end symbolises man's entry into the material world, and through baptism a return towards the re-birth of the spirit, the magical operation at the place of transformation, the altar. This is also reflected in the two towers on either side of the west door (the duality of the world), and the single central tower above the crossing (the light-filled unity of the spirit). (See 'pillar' and 'lantern'.)

The East as the source of wisdom and truth is found everywhere in fairy story and myth: the imagery is the same one, of a search for the light of divine intelligence and life-power embodied in the sun. (See 'west end'.)

EFFIGY

French *effigie*, from Latin *effigies*, 'likeness, portrait', which is associated with *effingere*, 'to form, fashion'. Thus the meaning of a figure fashioned to represent a person.

The figures at the feet of effigies have various significances. They may represent any enemy of the spirit, such as a serpent denoting evil, trodden underfoot, as in Eastern symbolism; they may have heraldic meaning or describe the subject by name or vocation; or they may be emblems of qualities, as the lion, strength, and the dog, fidelity.

In a church, effigies traditionally have their foot towards the altar, a reminder that in death all will be raised up to face Christ, the Judge.

EGG AND DART

A classical decorative motif on a moulding consisting of alternating egg and dart forms.

ELEPHANT

Latin *elephantus*, Greek *elephantos*, genitive of *elephas*. In the period of medieval wood-carving, the elephant, by virtue of its tremendous power, symbolised the majestic power of good over evil. It is found in stall work or bench ends, often with howdah upon its back.

68

EMBATTLE

Old French *bataillement* and *bastiller*, 'to fortify'. A figure used in heraldry and on Norman moulding resembling the parapet on a tower.

EMBRASURE

Old French *embraser*, 'to set on fire, inflame'. The word in architecture means the splay on the interior wall of a door or window, whereby the opening is wider on the inner than the outer wall. The reason for the use of the word is unknown.

ENCAUSTIC

Greek *enkaustikos*, 'burnt in'. Pavements and floor space in monastic institutions often have tiles where the colour has been fixed by a process of burning in. The effect was to produce something like a Roman mosaic – and the term tesselated (Latin *tesselatus*, 'composed of small stones') sometimes given to such tiles is innacurate. The arms of founders are often found on the tiles. The art of their manufacture seems to have been the prerogative of the monasteries, for they are not found elsewhere.

ENTABLATURE

Latin *tabula*, 'a table or board'. The whole of the horizontal superstructure lying upon a column in classical architecture. This is divided into three parts, as there are three major types of column (q.v.) and the column itself is of three parts – base, shaft and capital. The architrave is immediately above the capital, the frieze above that, and above is the projecting part or cornice.

EPISCOPAL

Latin *episcopus*, 'an overseer', from Greek *episkopos* (*epi*, 'over' and *skopos*, 'a watcher'). This is the word from which 'bishop' derives. The word episcopal signifies anything belonging to or vested in bishops, i.e. jurisdiction.

ESCUTCHEON

Old French *escuchon* (variant of *escucon*) from Latin *scutum*, 'shield'. *Scutum* is related to *cutis*, 'skin or hide' denoting the hide of which a shield is made. Thus the general meaning of a shield shape upon which coats of arms are depicted.

Latin *evangelium*, 'gospel', Greek *evangelion*, 'good tidings, gospel', (*eu*, 'good' and *angelia*, 'message'). The Evangelists are the writers of the four Gospels – Matthew, Mark, Luke and John. They are four in number because four is the number denoting the establishment of power on the material plane, as is seen in the symbolism of the four rivers in the Garden of Eden, the points of the compass, the solidity of the cube and so on. Each of the writers in his own way affirms and announces the incarnation of God as man.

The particular mode of expression of each Evangelist is related to the four elements through which the substantial universe manifests, and because incarnation is a fixing into a physical existence, each is related to one of the four fixed signs of the zodiac – air, fire, earth, water.

MATTHEW (Hebrew *Mattatiah*, 'gift of God') is related to Aquarius ♒ (air), because he evaluates as a man, sorting out the whole situation with clarity of memory and formal accuracy – he speaks of the human origins of Christ.

MARK (Latin, derived from *Mars*), is related to Leo ♌ (fire) because his energy is directed to authoritative statement – here is power, the power to draw men out of error, not mere statement.

LUKE (Latin name *Lucius*, from *lux*, 'light' – compare with the use of the word in 'Lucifer' (q.v.)) is related to Taurus ♉ (earth). His version is more intimate, more internal, and more on the material plane.

JOHN (Hebrew *Johanan*, 'God is gracious') is related to Scorpio ♏ (water). He is the odd man out – his is a version of visionary qualities that goes beyond the limits of the other three – in fact to the Higher Intelligence of the Logos.

Thus the Evangelists in Christian art, often found surrounding Christ in a window or at the termination of the limbs of a crucifix, take on the nature of the animals associated with these fixed signs:

Matthew – a man's head
Mark – a lion
Luke – a bull
John – an eagle

except that the eagle of St. John has replaced the Scorpion of the zodiac: he has assumed identity with the constellation Aquila, Eagle, which lies outside the zodiac. Why is this?

The change is obviously not an arbitrary one. It is because a passionate attachment to the world can become an equally passionate desire for a spiritual change – Scorpio is closely connected both with the sting of sexuality and with regeneration. (Such a regeneration is in fact prefigured in an earlier John, John the Baptist, who declared the possibility of it through baptism.) Consider, too, John the disciple whom Jesus loved for the sheer strength of his devotion. It is such intense devotion, epitomised in the sign Scorpio, that can lead ultimately to a break out from the confining circle of the temporal zodiac of the other Evangelists, into the eagle eye of simultaneous comprehension on the level of the Logos. It is for this reason that the extra-zodiacal constellation Aquila, the Eagle, has been attributed to John. (See 'eagle' and 'lectern'.)

These four 'beasts' are constantly depicted in iconography from an early date, surrounding Christ in Majesty or embellishing the ends of the arms of the cross, and their placing in the zodiacal sequence accounts for the order of the names as generally spoken – Matthew-Mark and Luke-John being pairs of opposites. Man is the central theme and purpose of creation and is correctly placed first, whilst the break out of the circuit of time is placed last as the ultimate achievement. The placing of the different symbols, however, has been arbitrary, even to the point of losing the natural heavenly sequence. In the version in the diagram the eagle rises above the head of Christ, suggesting the regeneration of man's sexual energies implied in the signs Taurus and Scorpio.

Thus one of the most commonly seen symbols in the church, and one of the least noticed, is seen to convey a wealth of meaning – a key to religious development. The fact that the four Evangelists and their symbols are archetypal spiritual powers is shown in their being represented with the wings of Cherubim: that the imagery is of great antiquity can be seen in the four-fold imagery of the sphinx of ancient Egypt. Here the head is of a man, the claws are of a lion, the body and tail are those of a bull, and the wings are those of an eagle. The higher aspects of these animals give the occult dictum 'know' (man), 'dare' (lion), 'keep silent' (bull) and 'do' (eagle). The imagery is also found in Ezekiel's vision of the creatures supporting the throne of God and in the four creatures of the Apocalpyse. (See Ezekiel I vs 5-10, and Revelation IV vs 6-8).

Whereas in the 5th century Byzantine artists depicted the Evangelists as half-man, half-beast, by the late Middle Ages in the West man and beast were separated, three of them with their respective animals by their sides. Often a scroll is used with each man or beast showing the initial words of each gospel. A representation of all four Evangelists in one animal (as in Ezekiel) is known as a 'tetramorph'. (See 'man', 'lion', 'bull', and 'eagle'.)

F

FALDSTOOL

Old High German *faldstool*, *fald*, 'to fold', and *stuol*, 'a chair'. Originally a stool or chair without arms, foldable and portable, for use by a bishop in a church other than his own. The term now applies to the desk to which a stool is attached and from which the litany is read. The litany desk faces away from the congregation, the priest addressing his prayer towards the altar.

FAN VAULTING

See under 'rib vaulting'.

FERETORY

Middle English *fertre*, 'shrine, tomb or bier'. Latin *feretrum*, from Greek *pheretron*, 'bier': all from Greek *pherein*, 'to carry'. Thus, a reliquary or casket containing the relics of a saint designed to be carried in a procession. The term is also applied to that part of a church devoted to such a shrine.

FIELD (in heraldry)

Old German *felt*, 'field, plain'. In heraldry it is the background of a shield – or of a given quarter of the shield upon which the charge is found. The field could be variegated in two ways – one, by 'powdering' (a scattered pattern of small charges of varying types) and, two, by subdivision with lines, some of which are extensions of the ordinary charges.

FIG-LEAF

Latin *ficus*, 'fig-tree', connected with Latin *fictor*, 'one who fashions or makes images'. The connection between the two words is found in the symbolism of the fig-tree as used in Genesis. The fruit of the fig-tree consists largely of seeds, and the fig-leaf Adam and Eve used to cover themselves in the story denotes the covering or loss of the inner creative power by the fall to the level of physical generation. The meaning is that from that moment the will of man was lost to the stimulus of the outer world epitomised by the woman. (See 'Adam and Eve'.)

FILLET

Latin *filum*, 'thread'. A small flat strip or band separating different mouldings and found in both classical and Gothic work.

FINIAL

Latin *finis*, 'end'. The upper projecting part of a gable or pinnacle; also the top of the decorated end of a bench or screen. They were especially employed along with crockets in the Decorated period.

FISH

'Fish' is one of many similar words, from a common Germanic root, of which one is Latin *piscis*, 'fish'. The fish as a symbol is closely connected with Christ. In the early Church he was called Iesoûs Ichthos (Jesus the Fish) or sometimes 'The Great Fish'. This was because Christ's birth heralded the beginning of the zodiacal era of 2,150 years, the Sign of Pisces (The Fishes). His disciples were known as 'fishers of men' and the early Fathers referred to their charges as *pisciculi*, 'little fishes'; the basin for washing the sacrificial vessels near the altar was a *piscina*, and the Greek word *ichthys* ('ιχθυς), 'fish', is made from the first letters of the words

73

Early oil lamp

Pisces

meaning 'Jesus Christ Son of God Saviour'; even the bishop's mitre (q.v.) is in form of fish's head, and in the New Testament we find the story of the Feeding of the Five Thousand with five loaves and two fishes and the feast on the shore of the Sea of Tiberius after Christ's Resurrection. The fish was a eucharistic symbol in early reproductions of the Last Supper and the elliptical aureole surrounding Christ in Majesty and later in the Middle Ages, the Virgin (q.v.), was called the *vesica piscis*, 'the bladder of the fish'. This is again a reference to the Piscean Age and to the illumination of the material 'sea' by the compassion of Christ.

The Piscean Era has much to do with the washing away of impurity, with renunciation and suffering, in order to make way for the new cycle of spiritual awareness, the Age of Aquarius. In terms of the individual, the image of the fish suggests the material and psychic sea in which a man flounders. But it is Christ descending into this sea, embracing all men in an act of sacrificial redemption, that shows the opposite face of Pisces. And man's confusion in the sea is redeemed by his own developing capacity for love and compassion.

FIVE WOUNDS

The five wounds are those made by the nails which fixed Christ to the cross – one through each foot and hand, and one made by the lance in the breast. They are generally seen as a symbol of the necessity of dying to the five senses. (See 'devil'.)

But the five wounds show man in a dual light. Five is a holy number in so far as it signifies the fully developed physical man, the last stage in his involution – spirit, as it were, reduced to perfected form. Such physical perfection is represented in the five senses and the five fingers that contact the outer world. But that form has developed along with, and at the cost of, an ego structure, an intellect, and an enslavement to the senses. Thus man as he is, stands at the cross-roads; is at a point of great power and yet great danger, for though the external aspects, it seems, rule his spirit, sacrifice can re-direct his spirit to higher levels. This is why 'five' is essentially to do with sacrifice, with the centre of the cross – the point of pinning – and yet of release.

The glyph of the number five is basically the cross of matter over the circle of spirit, as with the glyph of Saturn, but seen

Five

Saturn

Orb

74

in its redemptive light it is the reverse, the cross of the power of Christ over the world. (See 'orb'.)

The five petals of the rose convey the same meaning, for it is formally perfect, but the perfection on its negative side is a bewitching beauty that lulls the spirit to sleep – thus it is the Rosa Mundi, the Rose of the World, or the maya of creation. But the blood of conscious sacrifice (the thorns) awakens the Christ in a man and the rose is then the Mystic Rose, the new spiritualised world. Thus, the five petals represent in iconography the five wounds of Christ, and the red rose is often a symbol of Christ's sacrificed blood. (See 'rose'.) Similarly, the five pips of the apple form the five-pointed star, and the apple too (see 'Adam and Eve') signifies both the danger and the glory of the world.

The stigmata in art are those five wounds re-experienced in a physical sense by certain saints, as a result of their total dedication and sacrificial work. The five-pointed star is discussed under the heading 'devil'.

FLEUR-DE-LIS

A French word, 'flower of the lily'. It was the royal insignia of France from 1147. Originally completely covered by these flowers, from the time of Charles IV the banner consisted of three fleurs-de-lis on a blue field. The symbol occurs in English armorial bearing due to early English claims on French territory, and was featured as quartering in the English royal arms until the rule of George IV.

In the Church, due to the nature of the flower as a symbol, it was at an early time used in representations of the Annunciation and as a symbol of the Virgin Mary. (See 'lily'.) It is also seen at the termination of certain crosses, when it is either a cross-fleury or fleurée (a) or in diminutive, a cross fleurette (b).

a   *b*

FONT

Latin *fons*, 'fountain, source'. The word font is already used in Old and Middle English to denote the baptismal font, the carved stone or marble basin with lead lining used to contain the holy water for the sacrament of baptism. The part of the church where it stands is known as the baptistery. Fonts were of varying shapes in early Christianity, each symbolising some aspect of the meaning of baptism. In the 11th and 12th centuries the most common form was the tub without stem: it was only in the 12th and 13th centuries that the bowl was mounted on four legs, and only in the 14th that it had a single stem. These forms were related to the modifications that took place in the rite itself. In the earliest days of total immersion the rite took place in a space lower than ground level (symbolising also descent and re-birth), but when infant baptism began in the Middle Ages the font was raised for convenience to ground level, and later, when sprinkling was substituted, it became smaller and was raised higher on a pedestal. In these times, the consecrated water of the font was often stolen because of its magical properties, and it was as protection against this that fonts began to be covered. Originally plain covers, they eventually gave rise to the many beautifully carved, hanging, wooden canopies found in English churches.

The font is symbolic of two things – the fountain, the immaculate womb and source of matter in the form of the water itself; and the pure fire of the Holy Spirit, seen in the image of the dove (q.v.) which is often found above the font. These images are together because both aspects of man, the material and the spiritual, undergo symbolic regeneration in baptism. The whole meaning of baptism is to do with re-birth, and thus with the banishing of forces of evil, as medieval font carvings of serpents and griffins indicate. Re-birth became symbolised by the growing tradition of the octagonal font, number eight being the glyph for a new beginning. (It is a new octave formed by one circle leading out of another.) And, most important, the font is in the west end of the church building, either central or to the south side (heraldically left, the side of error), the entrance to the 'sea of life' as opposed to the potentially regenerated spirit at the east end. (See 'right and left' and 'east end'.) For the same reason, the number eight is also associated with the new dispensation – the turning point in the evolution of man following upon Christ's life on earth. And the cruciform church building, the vehicle of the dispensation, has eight angles.

FOUR DOCTORS OF THE CHURCH

The four Doctors or Fathers of the Church are often shown together in iconography: they are St. Jerome, St. Ambrose, St. Augustine and St. Gregory. Together they established the Church and its doctrines, and from the 10th century onwards were regarded as divinely inspired and infallible. They are four in number because four is the number of stability, of the establishing of power on earth as with the Evangelists (q.v.)

and such archetypal images as the four rivers in the Garden of Eden, the four points of the compass, and so on.

St. Jerome: born circa 342, ascetic and translator of the Old Testament and New Testament into Latin (The Vulgate), is seen either as a cardinal carrying a miniature church in his hand, or as an ascetic with wasted limbs and carrying a book and pen; also in the latter role sometimes with a lion in accordance with legend.

St. Ambrose: born 340, is seen with episcopal robes and with mitre and crozier, holding a book. A persuasive orator and advocate of asceticism, he is often seen with a bee-hive, after the story that a swarm of bees alighted on his mouth as a child and did him no harm. More frequently he has a scourge, an emblem of the severe penances inflicted by him upon sinners.

St. Augustine: born circa 354, was a great theologian and author of a monastic rule which subsequently gave rise to the order using his name. Above all, he made a system out of the strands of Christianity. His greatest work, and the first of its kind in literature, is 'The Confessions'. He is dressed as a bishop carrying a book.

St. Gregory: born 540, known as Pope Gregory the Great, was a reformer of Church liturgies and music, and a strong advocate of celibacy. He is represented as being of dark complexion with the tiara of a pope and a dove near his shoulder.

FRANCISCANS

One of the four main orders of friars (brothers depending on alms for support), known also as the Order of Friars Minor. They were founded by, and named after, St. Francis of Assisi circa 1209, and reached England in 1224. They were bound to poverty and gained respect for their scholarly achievements. Roger Bacon was a Franciscan. Because of their grey habits, they were known as Grey Friars.

FRATER, FRATRY, FRATERY

Old French *fraitur*, an abbreviation of Low Latin *refectorium*, 'refectory'. The dining room of a monastery. (See 'refectory'.)

FREEMASON

(Refer also to 'mason'.) Originally said to be a stone cutter who used a chisel as opposed to one who could only dress stone with cruder implements, or simply build walls. Thus the word is said to be a contraction of freestone-mason. (Freestone is stone that may be cut with relative freedom into blocks and then worked by chisel.) Due to the special skill of masons – those nameless artists responsible for beautiful windows and sculpture, and moreover the custodians of spiritual truths through their work – privileges were conferred upon them, for instance freedom of movement from country to country. In this sense the guild of masons enjoyed a liberty not entertained by other guilds.

Moreover the mason, both in his external trade and symbolically, was always the shaper of matter, and held a special place in the occult traditions of ancient civilisations. His secrets of structure were also concerned with the free spirit of man and its growth within the structure of the physical body. Thus the idea of 'free' occurs on various levels. It should be remembered too that the medieval cathedrals were built wholly on the sites: it was only after the plague at the end of the 13th century that the work of masons began to be done in 'shops', places distant from the building itself, as in the Wye Valley, and that work was transported from there to the site. This was just one of the many factors in the decline of medieval tradition, which culminated in the Reformation, the Dissolution of the Monasteries and the inner meaning of the masonic tradition itself.

FRESCO

Italian *fresco*, 'fresh', from the Old High German *frisc*. Painting on walls of churches during the medieval period was done with watercolour whilst the plaster was still wet – hence the term. This accounts for the durability of the colour so embodied.

FRIAR

French *frère*, Latin *frater*, 'brother'. A name given to a brother in one of the four mendicant orders – that is those orders depending on alms for their existence – the Dominicans, Augustinians, Franciscans and Carmelites. (See under each heading.) The original sincerity of such a dependence is demonstrated by the fact that certain of the orders were not allowed to receive money. All came to Britain at the beginning of the 13th century.

FRITHSTOOL or FREEDSTOLL

Anglo Saxon *frith* or *frid*, 'peace', plus 'stool'. A plain stone seat that used to stand in the sanctuary of certain churches affording sanctuary to criminals who reached it: the privilege was endowed by King Athelstan in 900 and not abolished until 1623. A sanctuary church boundary was determined by crosses outside the town. Once inside the church and seated on the frithstool, the criminal could not be seized. In the churches where the privilege applied, a priest was on watch and the well known sanctuary knockers (as the one at Durham) were used to gain entrance. The period of freedom was for forty days, after which serious offenders were obliged to leave the country. The records of Beverley Minster name hundreds of such sanctuary seekers, and it was the abuse of the privilege that finally led to its annulment.

FYLFOT

A word said to be a rendering of 'fill the foot'. It is used from medieval times to denote the swastika cross, the turning cross of great antiquity (q.v.). But in this context it denotes merely an ornament of classical antiquity in the form of the swastika which was used as an ornament for embroidery and sometimes in window decoration, thus filling the foot of cloth or window.

G

GALILEE PORCH

In medieval churches a porch at the west end so named was used as a chapel for penitents and those excommunicated from the Church. The name is said to derive from Latin *galeria*, 'a long porch'; but the many images of water belonging to the west end of a church (stoup, font, nave, porch) suggest that this name was probably used with reference to the Sea of Galilee and to the faith required to walk again upon the surface of the waters. Equally as Galilee was distant from Jerusalem, so the porch was at the furthest point possible from the sanctuary, the privileges of which were being sought.

GARGOYLE

Old French *gargouille*, 'throat', Latin *gurgulio*, 'gullet' or 'windpipe'. Thus the connection with the waterspouts spewing out rain from the gutters; and also, symbolically, by the aid of the grotesque animal or human heads, spewing out forces of evil from the house of God. Equally they can be seen as sentinels against evil forces attempting to gain entry. In many cases, though the mouths of the creatures are open, the water is conveyed through a lead spout above or below the figure.

GARDEN OF EDEN

Old High German *gart*, 'enclosure' and Eden, a Hebrew word meaning 'delight', signifying the innocence of man in his angelic state as body of light (de-light), before his involvement in the time process in the material world. Innocence means without harm (Latin *nocere*, 'hurt, harm'), and the light here implied is a different one to that of the diurnal light and dark.

The Garden is enclosed or guarded, and the expulsion from it is a deprivation of that protection through a misuse of the will, and an exposure to the physical world involving the division of the senses and the 'fall' described in Genesis. (The story in Genesis is an allegory of physical birth.) The involvement is at the same time a saving grace, a means of a man refinding his will, without which his error would have gone unchecked, assuming devilish proportions. The intuitive awareness, the unfallen state, is described as the Tree of Life, and the externalised awareness as the Tree of Knowledge from which Eve took the apple. Both these trees are depicted in church iconography.

The apple represents the whole world and the fulfilling of its purpose, in which case it is the golden apple of Greek mythology; it is also, negatively, the suffering incurred by man in becoming involved in the process – i.e. eating it when offered it by the serpent. Latin *malum* can mean 'apple' and 'bad', depending on pronunciation.

Also depicted in iconography is the quartering of the Garden of Eden by the four rivers described in Genesis. These rivers symbolise the archetypal division of energy from the one source. The lower planes are born of, and are constantly fertilised by, the higher, and appear first as the elements, fire, air, water and earth.

80

Pison – signifies joining and encompassing – the function of pure spirit: it is associated with a place where gold is found.

Gebon – signifies bursting into life.

Hiddekel – signifies light fluid movement.

Euphrates – signifies power which is fruitful.

On the subtle plane in the human being, the divisions are into: pure spirit (fire), etheric or life body, connected with laws of growth and with thought (air), astral or desire body connected with feelings and animal desire (water), and the physical body, subject to laws of the mineral world (earth). On the strictly physical plane, these become the nervous system (fire), the breathing system (air), the circulatory system (water), and the digestive system (earth).

(The symbolism is continued under 'Adam and Eve'.)

GENEVA BIBLE

See under 'Breeches Bible'.

GILBERTINES

An English monastic order founded by St. Gilbert of Sempringham, the monks following the rules of the Augustinians and the nuns (it was generally a mixed house) following the rules of the Benedictines. At the Suppression there were 26 houses in this country.

GLORY and CHRIST IN GLORY

Latin *gloria*, 'fame, renoun', from a base meaning 'to cry out, to sing', from which the Latin *gallus*, 'cock', really 'the singer'. It is the cock that heralds the day. And it is singing out, i.e. sound, that produces the world: Son is the same word as *son* (French) 'sound'. Sound and creation are one and the same: what has been created has been sung out. Thus in its present context it is both singing out in the joy of creation and the radiant light of divinity.

A glory is the name for the light radiating from behind God or Christ in iconography, embracing both the nimbus around the head and the aureole surrounding the body. It represents the perfectly functioning inner bodies of a man, purified of the opaqueness and distortions found in the unregenerated. It is used in representations of the supernatural events in Christ's life – the Transfiguration, the Risen Christ, the Ascension and the Day of Judgement. The clearly out-

lined elliptical shape is more specifically known as a 'mandorla' (q.v.). In sculpture, a 'Christ in Glory' is often found
from the 13th century in the tympanum above the west door.

GOSPELS

Old English *godspell*, from *god*, 'good' and *spell*, 'tidings',
Low German *spellen*, 'to say'. For Christianity, the good
tidings are the story of Christ as given by the four Evangelists,
Matthew, Mark, Luke and John. They constitute the first four
books of the New Testament. (See 'Evangelist'.)

GOTHIC

Latin *Gothus*, Greek *Gothos*, 'Goth' – a member of an
ancient Germanic tribe who in the 5th century overran the
greater part of the Roman Empire. The term as applied to
architecture has nothing to do with that tribe, but has come
to be used to denote the usurping of Roman style by an alien
style. Vasari, 16th century painter and architect, was the first
to use the term to describe buildings of the Dark Ages since
they were the result of the Gothic invasions and therefore
barbarous. Sir Christopher Wren used the term Gothic to
denote the later 'vandalising' of the classical purity of his
buildings. But broadly speaking the term is now used to
denote medieval architecture over the period from the 12th
to the 16th centuries.

The architecture of this period, of course, reveals a spiritual
strength diametrically opposed to the associations of the word
itself. The driving force behind it all was a sense of aspiration, for it would seem that the spirit could not fly high
enough in its endeavour to reach heaven, and this is embodied
in the external fact, the form of the cathedral. Architecturally
the change was from a rounded heaviness to a soaring height.
Key concepts were elasticity and balance, refinement and tension. A mason would tap a pillar to hear its tone, to assess the
correctness of its stress and strain. A cathedral was in this
sense a highly-strung balance of downward weight and upward thrust, a phenomenon reflecting the finely balanced
earthiness and spirituality of the period. Thus the problem
of vaulting, and the phenomenon of the buttress. Stone was
used in a completely new way and all apparent immobility
and heaviness due to gravity was somehow transcended. The
ribs of arches and the vaulting caused early writers to use the
image of the avenues in a forest, and to see the whole as a
flowering of the Tree of Life.

Gothic architectural style is for convenience divided into three periods, but styles overlap as in all such attempts at nomenclature; for instance, the end of the Early English and the beginning of the Decorated is not clearly definable. The following table gives two random interpretations, showing the problem:

EARLY ENGLISH	1189-1272	1189-1307
DECORATED	1272-1350	1307-1377
PERPENDICULAR	1350-1500	1377-1458

Overlapping of styles is best seen in the study of window tracery in its correspondence with the above periods. (See 'window'.)

GRAVEYARD

Grave is from Anglo-Saxon and Old High German *graf*, from Gothic *graba*, 'cave, trench, grave'. It now signifies an excavation made to receive a dead person or a monument marking a dead person. Gothic *graban* also means 'to carve' in the sense of engraving a stone, thus the modern meaning of incising or engraving.

Gravestones in parish churches are not found before the 16th century. Monuments for the wealthy were erected within the church and the poor had no monument. When it became necessary to extend monuments outside the church, there was obvious differentiation between rich and poor. Larger copies of the altar were called 'altar tombs', and those with sides open 'table tombs'. A simple slab on the ground is called a 'ledger'. It was mainly in the 18th century that there was imitation of classical themes – urns, sarcophagi and so on.

Due to the general symbolism of the points of the compass where the north is death both to the human spirit and in nature, it was a custom in medieval times to bury the bodies of suicides, reprobates and unbaptised children in the north side of the churchyard.

GRIFFIN

Latin *gryphus*, Greek *grupos*, 'curved, hook-beaked'. As a classical mythological beast, the griffin, with head, wings and talons of an eagle, and ears and body of a lion, is a symbol of vigilance. It has a combination of vigilant eye and courageous heart. In medieval times in the church, the negative aspects of the two creatures of prey made it the epitomisation of carnal appetites and evil.

83

GRISAILLE

French *gris*, 'grey', from a Germanic origin, plus *aille*, a Latin adjectival suffix. The name is given to a type of stained glass used in the 13th century which had a grey-green tinge, the object of which was to allow through a greater amount of light than the deeply stained windows permitted. The designs on these windows, as in the one at York Minster, consist of simple geometric patterns which became more complex and later incorporated foliage motifs.

GROINED VAULTING

Vaulting where the individual vaults cross each other at right angles: groining was used by the Romans and, when used by the Normans, simple ribs were added.

GUILDS or CRAFT GUILDS

Middle English *gilde* (from an Old Norwegian root), 'payment' or 'guild'. The word guild in the sense of a fraternity derives from the idea of payment for membership. Such fraternities, the fore-runners of Trade Unions, protected the interests of workmen against unjust masters, or the interests of masters against poor workmen. The guilds of the different crafts, already found in the 11th, and flourishing in the 13th and 14th centuries, were deeply involved in the business of erecting churches, and often advertised themselves in medallions in the windows of side-aisles or ambulatories. The religious guilds themselves – that is, fraternities devoted to the well-being of church members – met their end at the Dissolution of the Monasteries.

H

HAGIOSCOPE

Greek *hagios*, 'sacred', and *skopen*, 'to see'. See under 'squint'.

HALO

Latin *halos*, 'halo', Greek *halōs*, 'threshing floor'. On the threshing floor, oxen went round in circles – thus the connection with the circular form of the golden light surrounding the head of a divinity. It is also known as an aureole, glory or nimbus, but of these, the first two are used in error (q.v.).

It is hardly likely that this particular cyclic movement of the bull on the threshing floor should have been arbitrarily adopted. The bull, in this imagery, as in zodiacal symbolism, denotes the confirming of power to cyclic, mechanical repetition – to the prison of time. But the power, after transmutation, becomes the perfected and spiritualised 'solar body', the true life and light of a man, which on the subtle plane is seen as a radiating sphere of light enveloping the head.

HAMMER-BEAM

A beam which began to be used towards the end of the 14th century in a Gothic-style roof to strengthen it by diminishing the pressure falling upon the walls. Its characteristic is that it does not go straight across the width of the roof. The ends of the beams are often decorated with carvings, especially with angels bearing shields.

HAND

See 'Dextera Dei' and 'blessing'.

HATCHMENT

In heraldry, an abbreviation of 'atcheament', which is an early modern English word for 'achievement'. 'Achieve' is from a French word *achever* meaning 'to accomplish', from French *à chef venir*, and earlier Low Latin *caput venir*, meaning 'to come to a head.' Thus the word is to do with personal achievement and, heraldically, social classification through this. A hatchment is an escutcheon or shield painted on a square panel, at one time hung – with the points facing N, S, E, and W – on the front of the house of a land-owner to indicate death. It was later taken to be hung in the church with which that particular family was associated.

HEART BRASS

15th and 16th century church brasses show a heart, either alone or held in hands. It was not uncommon in those days for the hearts of men killed in battle abroad to be sent back for interment, and such an interment was recorded on the walls of churches by the 'heart brass'.

Middle English *herald*, Old French *heralt*, and derived from Old High German *harēs*, 'to proclaim': the second part of the word is from Old High German *waltan*, 'to govern'. Thus the meaning is the proclaiming the rights of government, as in the expression 'to herald' when a high official is announced. It only later signified the proclaiming of hierarchical precedence by means of emblems.

Heraldry began as signs or devices on the accoutrements of knights, especially shields, designating a particular family – a system developed in western Europe early in the 12th century, though emblems had been used nationally and personally in all civilisations. A means of being recognised in battle, pageantry, individual prowess, status in feudal life – all contributed to making an exact science of heraldry by the middle of the 13th century. All lords and many ordinary knights bore arms by this time. Combining of arms in one shield was originally caused through the union of two or more lordships or a wife's need to be distinguished from her husband.

By the 14th and 15th centuries, the needs of war had given way to the needs of family genealogies, and decorative tombs in churches show several generations of inter-marrying by quartering a shield and subdividing the quarters. Saints too acquired arms and emblems which often took the place of pictorial representation in the windows. Though symbolism was carried down in the emblems, much punning of names and other devices at this time began to make up the pictorial images.

The Royal shield of England truly established itself between 1154 and 1340 with three lions 'passant' (walking with one paw raised): this covered the reigns of Henry II, Richard I, John, Henry II and the three Edwards. These lions have withstood all change and exist in the present English shield: they are also referred to as leopards, since the French accepted the

| 1154 – 1340 | 1340 – 1405 | 1405 – 1603 | 1603 – 1714 | 19th century |

name lion only when it was 'rampant' (standing erect in fighting posture on its hind legs). From 1340, during Edward III's reign, quartering of the shield began, and from then until 1603 the French fleur-de-lis took precedence over the English lion, filling the 1st and 4th quarters. From the dating point of view, there are two periods – the first, between 1340 and 1405, has fleur-de-lis filling the whole space, but in the second, until 1603, there are only three in each quarter (known as 'France Ancient' and 'France Modern' respectively).

With the Stuarts, 1603 onwards, the previous arms were used, but, in the 2nd and 3rd quarters, the arms of Scotland and Ireland were added. Also at this time the 'supporters' of the shield became the familiar lion and unicorn, the unicorn taken from the Scottish shield. From the Restoration in 1660, it was made compulsory to display the Royal Arms in churches, and the subsequent variations are often found there. Only in 1801 was the French fleur-de-lis removed from the English shield, giving the present lion passant, the Scottish lion rampant and the Irish harp.

There are two mottoes found along with the arms: 'Honi soit qui mal y pense' (also the motto of the Order of the Garter), and 'Dieu et mon droit'. The first is usually associated with an anecdote in Edward III's life, but can be generally read as 'Evil be to him who thinks evilly on a thing' or 'Evil will come to him who thinks evilly'; and the second, the parole of Richard I before a certain battle, is literally 'God and my right', signifying God first and then his kingship, his individual will dependent upon God alone.

The study of heraldry is highly complex, but explanations of some basic terms – 'field', 'charge', 'blazon', 'escutcheon', 'hatchment', 'supporters' – will be found under their respective headings.

HERSE or HEARSE

Middle English *herse*, 'a moveable frame' over a tomb for holding candles or to take the cloth cover or pall. From Old French *herce*, 'harrow', the frame resembling the harrow in form. Such a wooden frame was part of the church furnishings and old ones have perished: however a few metal frames still exist on tombs.

HIBERNO-SAXON

'Hiberno' is from Latin *Hibernia*, 'Ireland'. The term refers to the admixture of the early Irish crude monastic style and

87

the indigenous style of the Saxons, which took place during the influx of Irish missionaries during the 7th century in Britain.

HIGH CROSS

Ireland, circa 900

Wales, circa 1000

The purely sepulchral slabs and monuments with a simple cross or monogram of Christ, which were found in large numbers in Ireland, died out in the 10th and 11th centuries, and in their place, vertical crosses, so called high crosses, began to be erected. The best examples belong to the 10th and 11th centuries and are the final flowering of that great period of Irish religion, learning, and art, which started in the 6th century. They are covered in elaborate sculpture showing scenes from the scriptures.

Whereas sepulchral monuments marked the resting place of the dead, the high crosses proclaimed the doctrines of the Church, giving a feeling of awe to the sacred ground where they stood. Most of the high crosses are in Ireland, but the Celtic influence is found in a few in Northern Ireland and especially in the Scottish standing stones and crosses which have a great delicacy in their ornamentation. Crosses in Wales and Cornwall do not have the same artistic merit.

HOG-BACKED STONE

A monumental stone placed horizontally over a gravestone which, because of its central ridge and sloping sides, gave the impression of a hog's back. They were usually about six feet long, carved with runes and designs typical of the period and had beasts' heads at one or both ends. Such stones are few in number and are found in Scotland and Northern England; they belong to the 8th and 9th centuries, the period of the commingling of Saxon and Irish cultures.

HOLY WATER

See under 'stoup'.

HOOD-MOULDING

Old English *hod*, from a Germanic base *had*, 'to protect', giving the word 'hat'. The stone moulding over a window or door acting to channel off the rain: it is also known as a 'dripstone'.

88

Latin *hostia*, 'sacrificial victim'. The Host is the consecrated wafer or bread which represents the sacrificed body of Christ, partaken by celebrants of the Eucharist. Partaking of it also implies the sacrificed body of all individual men united into one new body – the corporate body of regenerated man. (See 'Mass', and 'blessing'.)

HOUSELING BENCHES

Saxon *husel*, 'Eucharist, sacred bread'; Gothic *hunsl*, 'sacrifice', and other words associated with the meaning of holy. A houseling bench is a moveable wooden bench used before the introduction of altar rails. In pre-Reformation days it was placed before the communicants receiving sacrament and covered with a houseling cloth, the purpose of which was to prevent crumbs from falling to the floor.

I

ICON

Latin from Greek *eikon*, 'image, likeness, statue'. In the Church, specifically the Greek Church, it means a portrait of a saint or of Christ with the face of coloured enamel showing through a metal cover or superstructure. It is more generally any sacred likeness in the form of a statue or painting. Actual representations of Christ are not found until the 3rd century, the divinity of Christ being considered beyond representation. Early symbolic images of Christ as Orpheus soon gave way to the Shepherd, the Sacred Monogram and the Fish. Early representations of gems and lamps show Christ as a young man of classical beauty; it is only later in the 4th century that he was portrayed as an older figure, a kingly ruler with a halo, and in Byzantine art with a beard. His image was still however non-humanised, rather solemn and spiritual in feeling.

The Cross as the place of Christ's suffering did not appear in art until the 5th century, and Christ's body is always shown fully clothed until the 11th century. From the 12th century, the bearded Christ is universal. It was only with the Gothic period that he was portrayed as man suffering, naked and twisted, and only later, when man became the measure of all things that this suffering was sentimentalised in order to bring each individual into a relationship of suffering with him.

I.H.S.

See under 'monogram'.

ILLUMINATED MANUSCRIPTS

A translation from the Latin would be literally 'lit-up writing by hand': illuminated manuscripts are the equivalent of stained glass in the books of the monks of the medieval period, and have derived their name from the radiant effect of the gold used. As an art form, it came from a natural need to decorate and give free rein to the imagination. The original overspill into the margins finally lead to the fine miniature paintings which were one of the finest achievements of medieval art.

The religious zeal of the 6th and 7th centuries in Ireland produced much beautiful illumination, notable for the use of geometric design. Typically Celtic animal shapes, elongated and intertwined, were called 'lacertines' or lizards. The best known example of this period is the Book of Kells (8th century), also called the Book of Columcille because it was found in a monastery founded by that saint. Following this, in Northumberland, is the Lindisfarne Gospels or Book of St. Cuthbert, which had Byzantine suggestions in the figures due to the missionary flow between Britain and Rome after the time of St. Augustine. Ravages from attacking Danes ensued, destroying the Northern tradition, and King Alfred's stand against these invasions caused the art of illumination to flourish in Winchester, the ancient capital of Wessex. Here the famous Benedictional of St. Athelwold (end of the 10th century) was written: it had many departures from the Celtic and Celtic-Saxon style due to the influence of Carolingian art (the period beginning with and following the reign of Charlemagne, circa 770-900, where there was a return to the strictly Roman classical model).

From the Conquest until 1300, illumination, influenced by French work, continued in Canterbury, Bury St. Edmunds and at Peterborough. During the 13th century the demand for smaller copies of the bible increased due to the teaching friars, and as it did, so did the need for minuteness in the work. At the end of the 13th century, however, Paris had become the capital of miniature painting and remained so for a long time; but a change had come about. Hitherto it had been the monk who, labouring only for love, had spent much of his life illuminating his manuscripts, but now the lay-miniaturist, working for profit, had come into being. For instance, in Britain, in the well known Queen Mary's Psalter (14th century), the sacred themes have scenes in the margins of contemporary life, suggesting the work of a lay artist. There was now a profession of scribes and illuminators.

The 15th century was the apogee of miniature painting. Many secular works were done under patronage; but by the 16th century the work had become too elaborate, and the powerfully felt simplicity of the earlier centuries was gone. Also painting on canvas was now at its height and superseded the work of the illuminator.

IMPOST

Latin *impositum*, past participle of *imponere*, 'to place upon'; thus the horizontal moulding on the capitals on top of a pillar, pier or corbel upon which an arch is placed.

INDULGENCE

Latin *indulgentia*, 'gentleness, remission', *indulgere*, 'the act of indulging, the privilege of remission granted as a favour'. In the Church, the remission was of the pains of purgatory; that is, the punishments due for certain sins: they were granted for payments towards the upkeep and rebuilding of the cathedrals. Such indulgences were the source of revenue for many of the rebuilding operations after disasters to structure, whether by war or from natural causes.

INFIRMARY

In and Latin *firmus*, 'strong, robust': thus 'not strong'. In a monastery, a room used to house the sickly, usually located near the east end of the choir and on the south side. The infirmary itself has the long form of the church, the west end being the infirmary itself and the east end the chancel with altar.

IONIC (COLUMN)

From *Ionia* – part of ancient Greece having its own particular architectural style. The columns are of slender proportions: the capitals are decorated with volutes and the shaft is fluted. Contrary to the Doric, this column has a base. The column was based on the elegance of the female form as opposed to the rugged simplicity of the Doric. Often in Greece it was transformed into a Caryatid, a virgin bearing the burden of the pediment. The Ionic is the polar opposite of the Doric. Correspondingly, all the philosophers of the Ionic school (Thales, Anaximenes, Anaxagorus, Heraclitus) stress the material universe, aiming to establish that created things come from a universal physical source – water, air, atoms and fire.

I.N.R.I.
See under 'monogram'.

IRIS
See under 'lily'.

J

JACK-IN-THE-GREEN or THE GREEN MAN
A figure or face partially hidden in foliage, widely used in ornamental carvings in the medieval church. This was a representation of the beneficent spirit of vegetation or the tree-spirit, whose return to life was celebrated on May Day by the decking of a chimney sweep in a wicker framework covered with leaves and flowers.

On a boss

JACOBEAN
A term referring to work in the history of art produced between 1603 and 1625 during the reign of James I, whence the name arises. 'James' is a version of 'Jacob' (Jacob, Hebrew 'the supplanter'). Late Latin has '*Jacomus*', a version of Jacobus, which through many variants became James. The period also loosely extends beyond 1625, covering a style of heavy oak furniture, which characteristically has bulbous legs. Examples of Jacobean woodwork can be seen in many British churches.

JAMB

French *jambe*, 'leg', from Low Latin *gamba*, 'hoof'. The side post of a door or a window.

JESSE TREE or THE TREE OF JESSE

The tree of this name is found in medieval stained glass windows and illuminated manuscripts and is shown growing from the loins of a reclining figure. Jesse, the shepherd, was the father of David through whose line Christ was descended, and the Jesse Tree shows this lineage with the progenitors before the Babylonian captivity depicted as kings and those after it as patriarchs. Each progenitor is labelled by name at the termination of a branch of the tree and the Virgin Mary is at the summit with the Christ child in her arms. Symbolically, the stem does not touch the child, an indication of his divine incarnation. The tree depicted is usually a vine (q.v.) – the mystic vine, a symbol of spiritual fruitfulness. (There are examples of the tree with Christ crucified at the summit.)

The name Jesse denotes the affirmation of pure being (Latin *esse*), and in this sense the tree is the Tree of Life. The implication is that through the continuous work of many ancestors, a pure state of being is attainable, the prototype of which is Christ himself, born of a virgin, who is actually and symbolically a pure material vehicle. Though man's spiritual power has been reversed and now lies in his loins, that is in the form of sexual power used in a prone position, nevertheless it can undergo regeneration and recover its original function. This is the Christ state, potentially within all men, and the attainment of which is the aim of all religions.

JOHN THE BAPTIST

John the Baptist is frequently found in iconography in connection with the baptism of Christ. Distinguishable by his hairy apparel, John is the first of the three Johns in the New Testament – three aspects of love (*Johanan*, Hebrew 'grace of God'). He represents the working of the Holy Spirit within the physical body (hair), and the need to reverse its distorted values. John the 'beloved' disciple of Christ represents the devotion necessary in the feelings, the cleaving of the soul to what it knows to be Wisdom. John, the Evangelist, represents the potential break-out from the small logical mind, the yoke of cosmic forces and time itself, into a new dimension, and therefore has the symbol of the all-seeing eagle.

John the Baptist affirms the process of regeneration, proclaiming the birth of Christ as man on earth, and the potential birth of Christ in each man, a process which can only come about through dipping or washing in the Jordan to give a new order of life.

KEY

The etymology of the word is said to be unknown. However its meaning is bound up with the nature of the sound of the letter 'k': this is formed by the locking of the tongue to the roof of the mouth before release. The symbol of the key, though associated with several saints, belongs specifically to St. Peter, through the words in St. Matthew, 'And I will give unto thee the keys of the kingdom of heaven'; thus the key has come to represent the power vested in Peter and subsequently in the Church itself.

But this statement contains the paradox of the key, for it can both lock and unlock; it has two aspects, and Peter's keys are crossed (one silver and one gold) diagonally to show this. The power of God has become locked in the physical world, but that power can be unlocked. Individual man, full of error and locked into a physical body (the fall), may find his way back to freedom through the structure of the Church. But the Church is a formal structure and stands in danger of being a locked system; Greek *petros*, 'stone', may be a corner-stone, but it is also very hard. The secrets of life and death are bound in the physical world – in time and space. Peter holds the keys, but it is in the inner temple, through the unfolding of the Christ within, that the true key to the release from its tyranny lives. Thus the symbol of Peter is often of crossed keys over an inverted cross, indicating the need to reverse power invested in and directed to the physical world.

The locking and unlocking is seen most clearly in the field of music. Music is written on clefs (French *clef*, 'key') and has its own particular key. This is because matter is in effect condensed vibrations – all that lives has its own frequency. Sound in fact is a creative force. It is only necessary to find that frequency, and to resonate a given form by an outside stimulus of the same frequency – i.e. a musical note – to be able to destroy that form. Thus the locking of music in musical notation and its power to reach back behind the physical appearance are opposite poles. Such power in music was understood and used in the early Church. (See 'organ' and 'choir'.)

The Knights Hospitallers were originally concerned with caring for pilgrims at the Holy Sepulchre in Jerusalem. Their name derives from the hospices they maintained – 'hospice' is from Low Latin *hospitium*, 'hospitality' or 'inn'. The alternative name derives from St. John the Almoner, Patriarch of Alexandria in the 7th century, who aided Christians after the fall of Jerusalem into Saracen hands. For various reasons, the revenues of the community increased after the First Crusade in 1099 and the then head of the community offered to fight against the Mohammedans. Thus the order was divided into three classes: knights of noble birth who were to be soldiers, priests who were to remain in the Church, and serving brethren who were to be ordinary soldiers.

Originally they wore a black robe with a white linen cross on the left breast, but later it was decreed that whilst on military duties they should wear over this a red military greatcoat with a white cross.

The order came into Britain early in the 12th century.

KNIGHTS TEMPLARS

An order of monks based upon using force of arms in the protection of Christian pilgrims during the period of the Crusades. It was founded in Jerusalem in A.D. 1118 and declined in importance upon the evacuation of Palestine in 1291. The name Templars is derived from the fact that the house in which the order originated was near the Dome of the Rock, the mosque built upon the site of the Temple of Solomon.

In the beginning the Templars dedicated themselves to a life of extreme hardship and purity, but later they wielded much power through property (9,000 castles in Europe in the 13th century): their hierarchy ranged from the knight down to the craftsman. The order came to Britain in the 12th century, their church in London still remaining. Many of the churches were round in form, others polygonal. (See 'church'.)

L

LADY CHAPEL

A chapel dedicated to the Blessed Virgin in cathedrals and churches, usually found at the extreme east end behind the high altar but sometimes projecting from the main building. (See 'Virgin Mary' for symbolism.)

LAMB

German *lamn*, connected with Greek *lambda*, (the letter l, λ) and Hebrew *lamed* (the 12th letter of the Hebrew alphabet).

The image of the lamb figures frequently in Christian art, on missals, tympani, capitals, and so on. It represents Christ as 'the lamb sacrificed from the foundations of the world'. This sacrifice is that of the innocent white victim – God limiting himself through manifestation – the sacrifice of the one for the many. Manifestation is in the natural world, which can only perpetuate itself through a process of mutual eating, through one life being sacrificed to another: in this sense all things are mutually dependent. The ultimate sacrifice is God's sacrifice of Himself as Jesus Christ the man, so that all men may feed on Him; this is the essential message of the Eucharist where it is said that a man's sins are 'washed away by the blood of the Lamb'.

The idea of sacrifice is expressed in the Greek *lambda* λ which, when super-imposed over *gamma* γ (letter G), gives the six-pointed star, the wheel of Being, the Logos. In the illustration, John the Baptist holds the book with the lamb upon it, a double image of the Spoken Word and the sacrificed Son of God.

15th century window, All Saints: York

The Hebrew connection is through the letter *lamed* ל which contains the idea of sacrifice in its symbolism, for in its corresponding 12th card of the Tarot, the image is of a man hanging upside down. Conscious sacrifice is a hanging upside down of all worldly values; for when man is born into a physical body his power is inverted. The lamb is also seen in the sacrifices of the Paschal Lamb of the Hebrews, Easter being the celebration of the delivery of the Israelites from the Egyptians (symbolically spirit from the bondage of matter) by the smearing of the blood of the lamb on their door posts.

In iconography, prior to 683, the lamb is a symbol of Christ, often bearing the chi-rho monogram or a cross upon its forehead. The representation of Christ as a man was only allowed after the year 683, when the Council of Constantinople decreed 'We pronounce that the form of Him who taketh away the sins of the world, the Lamb of Christ our Lord, be set up in human shape, or images, henceforth, instead of the formerly used **Lamb**.'

96

LANCET WINDOW

Latin *lancea*, 'a light spear'; thus a narrow pointed window especially associated with the Early English period. The one at the east end of the church behind the altar symbolises the male spirit, raised out of the material world – the west of the church. It should properly portray the risen Christ rather than Christ crucified. (See 'east end' and 'Crucifixion'.)

LANTERN

Latin *lanterna*, 'lantern', Greek *lamptēr*, 'light, torch'. The lantern is the open structure at the top of a tower in a church; in a cathedral it is the central tower over the crossing which allows the centre of the church to be illuminated (See 'crossing' and 'transept' for symbolism.)

LAST JUDGEMENT

The Last Judgement is a common theme in medieval art. In it the 'wicked', those who have continued in a direction of error, are shown being consigned by Christ to the fires of Hell on his left, and the 'righteous', those who have taken the road of spiritual re-birth, are shown being drawn into Heaven on his right. An angel holding a sword sometimes separates the two or St. Michael may be seen weighing souls in the scales.

Due to the literal interpretation of 'a thousand years', in Revelation, there was among early Christians an expectation of the Second Coming, the Last Day when all would be held to account; but though this had not materialised by the end of the first millenium, the dread of the Final Judgement continued, and representations of it found their way into prominent places in the church building, as in the tympanum of the medieval cathedral, particularly in France. Such a message over the main west portal was a reminder of the destiny of all men. In the centre of the representation is Christ as judge in a mandorla (q.v.). The imagery was carried through into the parish church in the 'doom' (q.v.), often painted in pre-Reformation times in the filled-in space between chancel and rood-screen.

Christ as judge is prefigured in the Egyptian Osiris, and both cull the harvest of the work of man on earth. The idea of the unfolding and folding back upon itself of a process is inherent in the Alpha and Omega glyphs (q.v.). The idea of judgement is contained in the book, the Book of Life, which

Christ often holds upon his left knee, and from which nothing is left unrecorded. This judgement shows the ultimate triumph of good over evil where all error is consumed by the fire of the spirit, and a New Jerusalem is established. As far as an individual man is concerned, however, though he is said to be judged, it is his *own* record that is laid bare before his own gaze.

Such a judgement recurs constantly in man's earthly incarnations, for through the fascination of the world, the maya of existence, he is blind to his state in the spiritual worlds. He regains that eye of self-knowledge upon death only, when each element is filtered out so to speak and goes to its own place. In this sense he constantly judges his error and accumulates the fruit of his work in each life in readiness for the final liberating of his real Self. But despite the forces of the world, the real Self lives in every moment of time, capable of separating truth from falsity: it is an eye of real truth, not moral judgement. In this sense a man's work is to develop this eye, this awareness, so that his life is a constant rehearsal for death – a separation of his own sheep and goats.

LAST SUPPER

The word 'supper' is from Old Norwegian *supa*, 'to drink, sup'; compare with Sanskrit *supas*, 'broth'. The word 'sop' (the sop handed by Christ to Judas) is related to sup, and is simply the cake of bread soaked in the communal dish, the custom of the East.

Representations of the Last Supper are second only in number to the Crucifixion. The passing on of Christ's power through the shared bread and wine, and the subsequent shared meals of the early Christians (the *agapē*, Greek 'love') was to become the Lord's Supper, the sacrament of the Holy Eucharist (Greek *eukharistia*, 'thankfulness' from *eu*, 'good' and *kharis*, 'grace'). It is represented, in this light, on the altarpiece or reredos in the church – a scene of awe-ful solemnity; whereas elsewhere in art the treatment is more dramatised, with the stress on Judas' betrayal. No representation of the Supper is known in art before circa A.D. 800, and those to which we are now accustomed are misleading on a factual level, for the Jewish custom of the time was for meals to be taken in a reclining position upon the floor, resting on couches around the three sides of a low table. The Latin name for the couches, of which the central one was the seat of honour, is *triclinium*.

The significance of twelve apostles is treated under the heading 'apostle'. The significance of the mystical supper is discussed in part under 'Mass'. The bread and wine are basically the substantial body of God, the whole universe, and the life force that animates it: and, in that universe, life can only continue by a ruthless process of mutual eating. In man, microcosm of that universe, the blood is the medium of the life force, the mediator between spirit and body, and acts in either of two ways. Either it surges in anger, producing a state of disease, or it flows evenly and harmoniously, giving a state of health. The first is the state of fallen man, full of hate and bestiality, and the second is that of the regenerated man, who through sacrifice has surrendered his lower self, and who through love relates himself again to the whole world – to the *whole* Man. Jesus Christ is the perfect Being, human and divine, and his sacrificial act of shedding blood, foreshadowed in the Supper, allows his power in a sense to be eaten. He is the God who is being eaten by humanity in order that the earth should be re-spiritualised. He has made something available. Thus, the taking of bread and wine at the Sacrament is essentially an individual man's act of self-remembering, a joining of his separate self to the whole. Christ's gift is only available at the place where a man has made his own sacrifice, that is internally, in his heart, before he reaches the external altar of the church. To make this sacrifice is each man's own private drama, and the three central figures in the Lord's Supper correspond to parts of himself, for the apostles, through their respective natures, each fulfilled a special and conscious role. They are John, Peter, and Judas. John is portrayed on one side of Christ, intimately close to him, with Peter on the other side, whilst Judas is portrayed on the near side of the table or moving out of the picture having received the sop. Of these three only John is not found wanting.

The reason is that love, always associated with John (John, Hebrew *Johanan* means 'Jah is gracious') is the only total way by which that Christ power may be received. Utter selfless devotion brings about the wisdom of the Logos. (For this aspect of John see also under the heading 'Evangelists.') Peter (Greek *petros*, 'a rock, stone') on the other hand represents the hard knowledge in us, the seeing without feeling. Such clear-sightedness and dedication may set up the Church, but it can soon deteriorate into the hair-splitting wars over dogma. Judas (Hebrew, strangely meaning 'praise') represents the vulnerable part in man – the capacity to betray what the spirit knows as truth for the smallest selfish gain. Moreover, Judah, the same name, is the land of the Jews from which the word Jew derives, and it was they who rejected the inner message of universal love offered by Christ because their hope of a temporal and a personal King had not been fulfilled. Thus, psychologically and historically Peter and Judas are dangers. Christ knew he was to be apprehended, and could have been found at any time. The role of Judas was the most difficult to play: Christ's instructions to him are unequivocal, and the offering of the sop (such a gesture coming at a crucial point in the ancient 'mysteries') underlined the bitter acceptance of his role. He was to take the scorn of men of the spirit, as Christ took the scorn of the ignorant.

LAVATORY

Latin *lavare*, 'to wash'. In a monastery, a lavatory is usually a long stone trough at the entrance to the refectory where monks washed their hands before eating.

LAY BROTHERS or CONVERSI or FRATRES CONVERSI

'Lay' is from Old French *lai*, Latin *laicus*, Greek *laikos* 'belonging to the people' (*laos*, 'people'). A member of a monastic house under vows of celibacy and obedience but who is exempt from the studies and the musical activities of the monk. Thus the meaning of *'conversi'* – someone of the people who has undergone conversion and who has put himself under the vows of the monastery.

LECTERN

Middle English, from French *lettrum*, from Low Latin *lectrum*, 'reading-desk'. The lectern is the desk upon which the Bible rests and from which the lessons are read. Over it frequently presides the figure of an eagle (q.v.), which by its soaring flights and powers of sight symbolises the Logos, the Word and Intelligence in which all things are simultaneously embraced.

Thus the lectern is on the south side (heraldically the left) as opposed to the minister in the pulpit, God's mouthpiece, on the north side (heraldically right). The Word is manifest in the form of the Bible, and is specifically associated with St. John because, of all the gospels, his is the spirit that transmutes the written letter and touches the new dimension of the Higher Intelligence. This is also the case with man, for the break-out from the confines of the small, cutting, logical mind, bound by time and duality, is into the Higher Logic, a new dimension where all parts are seen in relation to one whole.

The eagle in relation to the four symbolic animals of the four Evangelists is discussed under 'Evangelist'. In a monastery, a lectern is often corbelled out of a wall in the refectory, and it was customary for readings to be made while the monks were eating.

LIERNE VAULTING

French *lien*, 'tie, bond'. In vaulting of the 14th century, a short cross-rib – i.e. one that does not spring from the wall but crosses from rib to rib. This produces intricate patterns known as 'stellar vaulting'.

LIGHT

Old High German *licht*, connected with Latin *lucere*, 'to shine'. The actual apertures in a wall through which light passes, as opposed to the whole concept of a window itself. Thus a window may consist of three or any number of lights.

LILY

Latin *lilium*, Greek *leirion*, 'lily', connected with Greek *leiros*, 'pale, delicate'. In Christian art the lily is a symbol of the chastity and purity attributed to the Virgin Mary: the Angel Gabriel is represented holding a lily in his hands at the Annunciation. In the crown of King Solomon, the lily denotes kingly and perfect love. In this sense, it is connected with the *Lila* of Hindu philosophy where the word signifies the play or game of God – a play opposed to the groaning struggle of man on earth. (This effort-ful struggle and its fulfilment, the flowering of beauty out of imperfection, is symbolised by the rose.) Where the lily is found, there is always the meaning of love shown from higher to lower, as with the Angel Gabriel's role of divine messenger to man; also Greek *iris* (the flower, the iris, is often substituted for the lily) means 'rainbow', which was symbolically a sign of reconciliation between God and man, as in the story of the Flood.

Due to the association of the Crucifixion and the Annunciation – both being celebrated around the spring equinox –

and since both are essentially acts of divine grace, there are a number of instances in wood-carving and window decoration showing Christ crucified over a lily plant. This is a peculiarly English device.

LION

Greek *leon*, probably from a Semitic origin – i.e. Hebrew *lābi*, 'lion'. In Christian art, the lion is the sign of the Evangelist Mark, who in his manner of writing exemplifies the qualities of Leo, the fixed fire sign of the zodiac. This archetypal image of the lion denotes energy establishing itself in a self-authoritative way, and on its highest level denotes courage, strength and love. It is these qualities that make the all-conquering Christ to be seen as the Lion of the Tribe of Judah in the Book of Revelation.

But the real inner power of the lion has given way to misused power – the animal passions in man have brought about the debased, devouring aspect of the lion within him. Energy has to be transformed and the true lion re-found so that ultimately, led by the Christ child, it can lie down together with the lamb, symbol of the innocent state of man. This is the divine state in man, when self-authority can be handed willingly into the hands of the Creator.

LLAN

The Welsh word for 'church', and prefixed to many Welsh place names. Originally it was a piece of ground – a sacred enclosure granted to a priest.

LYCHGATE or LICHGATE

A combination of 'gate' and Old English *lic*, Middle English *lich*, 'a body whether alive or dead'. The Old German counterpart and modern German *leiche* means 'corpse'. The lychgate is the gateway with a roof at the entrance to the churchyard where the coffin rests awaiting the arrival of the officiating clergyman prior to interment.

LOUVRE or LOUVER

Old French *lovier*, Medieval Latin *lodium*. The meaning was originally of a simple opening over a fireplace. The lantern or tower of medieval buildings was designed with sloping boards, called louvre boards, so as to let out the smoke, let in light and also keep out the rain. Thus the angles of the boards in a belfry window in churches are sloping to fulfil this function.

LOZENGE

French *losange*. A diamond-shaped figure used in heraldry and as a moulding in Norman architecture.

LUCIFER

Latin *lux*, 'light', and *fer*, from *ferre*, 'to carry, bear'. In popular understanding, Lucifer is the epitomisation of evil, a spiritual being responsible for the fall of man, but his name indicates, as the word tells, 'bringer of light'. He is both at one time, because fire and light are the pre-condition of creation, and creation itself is in a sense death, since power is locked into each specific life-form created. In this sense, Lucifer, the morning star (in fact, the planet Venus) is a cause of mourning, since not only does each day bring light and life, but it opens up the circus of painful existence once again. (See 'cock'.)

This duality, Lucifer's high estate and awe-inspiring fire of creation, and the prison of the world resulting from his intellectual pride, causes him to be represented as a being of deceptive beauty and as a hideous serpent. Satan, similarly, is in one sense a positive creative power, but he is also a negative limiting one, and this the planet Saturn's rings and the god Saturn's connection with time indicate. Equally, the devil is a negative aspect of God the Creator, for 'devilish' signifies that which is orientated to material inertias as opposed to the spirit from which it derives.

The serpent, associated with all three, crawls on its belly and is full of wile and evil intent; but it is at the same time the storehouse of that great power which awaits regeneration, seen in the symbolic casting of the skin: it is a healing agent as well as a force of evil. Such dialectics expressing dualism in the world abound everywhere.

LUNETTE

French word meaning 'little moon'. The word is applied to objects or designs having a small circular, semi-circular or crescent shape. Architecturally it refers to an opening in a vaulted roof, the purpose of which is to let in light.

M

Majesty is from the same base as Latin *magnus*, 'great'. The name in Christian iconography refers to a sculptured figure or painting of Christ, seated enthroned, crowned, and in an act of benediction. He is often in the presence of the apostles and surrounded by a mandorla (q.v.). The apse dome and the tympanum over the west door were the two places in the church used most often for showing off such a powerful image.

MAGI

'Magi' is plural of Latin *magus*, from Greek *magos*, 'a Persian priest; a magician'. There are many legends about the three kings or wise men who, it is said, foretold the birth of Christ and followed the star to where it took place. They were in fact not numbered until Origen, and not named until after the 6th century. Such astrologer wise men would certainly know the connection between the heavenly bodies and momentous happenings on earth. But their significance lies in that they symbolise the basic three-fold nature of man. It is three 'kings' who foretell the birth and pay homage, which indicates that this is a happening destined to transform the three fallen parts of a man's being, re-installing the divine authority (the kings) in each. This can be seen either in terms of man's whole evolution, or in terms of one man's lifetime. Thus, the significance of the gifts they bring.

Balthasar (Persian 'war council'), shown dark-skinned, represents the physical body, his gift being myrrh, connected with embalming and the sacrifice of the body; *Caspar* (Persian 'treasure-master'), shown yellow-skinned, represents the soul, his gift being that which affects the life of the feelings or soul, frankincense; *Melchoir* (Persian 'king') shown white-skinned, whose gift is gold, represents the pure intelligence of the Logos. As kings and Gentiles, as opposed to the Jewish shepherds, they also mark the new dispensation – the fact that the birth was a gift to all men for all time.

The form of the cross was used originally by the Knights called the Hospitallers of St. John, whose work at the time of the Crusades was to tend sick pilgrims in Jerusalem. It is an eight-pointed cross said to symbolise the eight beatitudes in Matthew. It is thus essentially an emblem of love. Later the order became more military, and finally, expelled from Rhodes by the Turks, settled in Malta in the early 16th century, whence the name.

The cross is found over Norman doorways and sometimes in the tympanum. It is often miscalled a 'pattée cross' (q.v.), a cross whose arms have flat terminations.

MAN

Old High German *man*, and related to Sanskrit *manus*, 'human being'. The *ma* part of the word indicates that he is born of the matrix or womb of matter and the plural form 'men' indicates his involvement in the mental process of measuring and counting (Latin *mens*, 'mind, reason', also *mensis*, 'month', and *mensura*, 'measure' etc: also see under 'Amen'). Thus the duality implicit in his situation as a being who can see and reason about his own physical involvement in the world.

In Christian art, the head and the other animals of the fixed signs of the zodiac symbolise the four Evangelists (q.v.). The head, as in the diagram, corresponding to the fixed air sign Aquarius, is the symbol of Matthew. The sign is concerned with memory and assimilation of information for unification into a whole, for the ultimate goal of man is that he should see all diversity in the material world as having a common origin, so that he may be drawn together with his fellows into one whole Man. Thus the significance of the forthcoming Aquarian age.

MANDORLA

The Italian word for 'almond'. The mandorla is the almond-shaped line drawn around the full-length figure of Christ, usually with fine lines radiating outwards from the body, showing the perfected inner light of divinity. The treatment varies according to the medium, whether it is sculpture or painting. The mandorla is associated with Christ of the Last Judgement, and especially with Christ in Majesty, though later, in medieval times, it became common to depict the

Virgin Mary in the same way. Another name for it is the 'mystic almond'.

The image of the almond is a reference to the fruit of the tree which by its form suggests the womb, thus the womb of the world from which all developed and within which the redemptive power of Christ operates. The almond tree is itself associated with purity of birth. In Arabic, the word means 'to waken' since it is the first tree to awaken in early spring with its white blossoms.

The mandorla is also known as the *vesica piscis* (Latin, 'bladder of the fish'), again an image of the waters of the womb of the world within which the Christ power radiates. In this sense Christ is the 'Great Fish' in the sea, having descended into that sea to redeem floundering humanity. (See under 'fish' for its symbolism.) Sometimes the mandorla is referred to as an *ichthus*, Greek 'fish', and again simply as the 'aureole' (q.v.). It is exclusively the property of Christ and the Virgin.

MASON

Said to derive from a Germanic base *mak*, 'to make'. 'Make' can be taken on two levels, internal and external. The masonic teaching goes back to the earliest civilisations and has the basic idea of building an inner, regenerated body out of the fallen physical one. This is the inner meaning, and in this sense the word 'mason' can be seen as 'son of ma', that is 'son of substance'. This denotes that a man can consciously shape or make the course of his life – that he is no longer shaped by the forces external to him. He is reborn out of his substance.

These external forces under man's control are symbolised by him standing within the cube looking out onto its three pairs of faces – above-below (cosmic forces and the earth), before-behind (duality of future and past), right-left (the doubleness of rational thought, yes and no), all of which symbolise the limitations of the world. But, when the cube is unfolded so as to remain in one piece, it becomes the Latin cross of Christianity upon which man is transfixed. If the process is reversed, and these limitations are transcended on the cross through sacrifice, then the cross folds back into the cube and becomes a true corner-stone for a new edifice.

It is not surprising therefore that, on all counts, the Latin cross should have been used in the external work of the builder, and that the cathedral should have symbolised that inner work. Masons were the holders of inner and outer

Fold on the dots

secrets, and the religious aspirations of medieval times came to a head in this co-joining of outer form and inner meaning.

Also, as men sensitive to the field forces of the earth, master builders aimed to increase the efficacy of their buildings as places of prayer by precise siting. Recent investigation has done much to confirm this aspect of the siting of most major religious buildings. (See under 'freemason' and 'mystery play'.)

MASS

The celebration of the Holy Communion in the Western Church, from an early time, has been known by the name 'Missa', which supposedly became 'Mass'. It is said that the word 'Missa' came from 'Ite missa est', an injunction to cate-chumens, those being instructed in early Christianity, to go at a certain part of the service, the remainder of the service being for the initiated: and that it was later used for all the faithful at the end of the service. The words could mean 'Go, the assembly is sent away', or 'Go, the Mass is ended.'

The focal point of the Holy Communion however is the symbolic partaking of the body and the blood of Christ, and it is more likely that the significance of the words lies in the connection with Old English *maessa*, 'feast', and Italian *messa*, 'a course at table', both of which are connected with French *masse*, 'barley-cake', which in turn is from *massein*, 'to knead'. The link throughout is the basic one of eating, and in such a fundamental ritual it is likely that the inner meaning would become embodied in the word adopted.

The key to the Mass lies in the reciprocal feeding by which all levels of beings in the world subsist. From spiritual beings down to the microbe, life is possible only by eating and then being eaten by another. This is apparent enough in nature, and even psychologically human beings feed upon each other, the stronger absorbing the weaker and the weaker gaining meaning from surrender to the stronger.

But 'as above, so below'; the same holds in the spiritual world. On the level which concerns us, Christ's sacrifice is literally food for the soul of the whole race of Man – at this particular time in evolution, a real spiritual food, the body and blood, has been made available which is represented by the bread and wine in the sacrament of the Eucharist. But the truth of man's situation is that in his fallen state he is poor food for a higher Being; by his state he impedes the working of the spiritual hierarchy, and, to alter his condition so that higher food is useful to him, he must first clear his own error. In short, religion, or the process of 'binding back' (Latin *ligare*, 'to bind'), is a reciprocal relationship – he has to recommit his will, to offer himself for use by higher levels. (See further under 'altar'.)

Historically, the Mass underwent many changes. Originally it was administered to the church members by the clergy, and this held in Britain until after the Norman Conquest. Medieval times however saw the separation of clergy from laity, the mystery in the sanctuary from the people, so that in the end, except on the death bed or on rare occasions, the Mass was celebrated vicariously, and focussed around the raising of the host for adoration. In 1546, Henry VIII commanded that the Mass should be a 'Communion' in which all should participate. Thus the dropping of the word 'Mass' in the Reformed Church, and the distinction between the chalice and the communion cup (q.v.).

The setting to music of the liturgy, which developed into the 'mass' as found in Palestrina and Byrd, and later into the 'Concert Mass', derived from five passages (the 'Ordinary' or 'Common' of the Mass) originally sung by the congregation in response to five passages of plainsong sung by the priest. These five passages gradually became more elaborately treated and were sung by chorus and soloists. They are:

KYRIE	Lord have mercy
GLORIA IN EXCELSIS	Glory be to God on high
CREDO	I believe
SANCTUS	Holy, Holy (the Benedictus is really part of the Sanctus, but is often treated separately)
AGNUS DEI	Lamb of God

In the later Protestant settings – of Bach, for example – these sections were subdivided to give the possibility of a more varied musical experience, and this later gave a Mass which was more of a vehicle for a composer's skill, rather than for devotion. Thus originated the 'Concert Mass', performed without the original liturgy from the priest. The five subdivided sections of Bach's B minor Mass (the first great example of such a Mass), are as follows:

KYRIE ELEISON	Lord have mercy
CHRISTE ELEISON	Christ have mercy
KYRIE ELEISON	Lord have mercy

LAUDAMUS TE	We praise thee
GRATIAS AGIMUS TIBI	We give Thee thanks
DOMINE DEUS	Lord God
QUI TOLLIS PECCATI MUNDI	Who takest away the sins of the world
QUE SEDES AD DEXTRAM PATRIS	Who sitteth at the right hand of the Father
CREDO IN UNUM DEUM	I believe in one God
PATREM OMNIPOTENTEM	Father Almighty
ET IN UNUM DOMINUM	And in one Lord
ET INCARNATUS EST	And was incarnate
CRUCIFIXUS	Was crucified
ET RESURREXIT	And rose again
ET IN SPIRITUM SANCTUM	And I believe in the Holy Spirit
CONFITEOR UNUM BAPTISMA	I confess one baptism
SANCTUS	Holy
HOSANNA IN EXCELSIS	Hosanna in the highest
BENEDICTUS QUI VENIT	Blessed is He that cometh
AGNUS DEI	Lamb of God
DONA NOBIS PACEM	Give us peace

MAUSOLEUM

Mausoleum, from Greek *Mausoleion*, a tomb erected by Queen Artemisia at Halicarnassus in Turkey in 353 B.C. to contain the body of her husband Mausolos. This tomb was one of the Seven Wonders of the World: thus the word is used to describe any great sepulchral monument.

MAZE

Middle English *masen*, 'to confuse, puzzle'. In some cathedrals, particularly on the Continent, a maze was designed on the floor of the nave – a symbol of the soul's entanglement in matter and the necessity and possibility of finding a way out of it. (The *ma* part of the word denotes matter, and the letter 'z' denotes the zealous buzzing about of the entrapped soul trying to free itself.) In some cases the mason's name was known to have been engraved upon them.

MENSA

The upper slab of an altar. At the consecration of the church, five simple Greek crosses were engraved into the altar, a reflection of the symbolism of the 'five wounds of Christ' (q.v.). These may be seen in churches where the original slab has been preserved.

The meaning of the name Michael is given under 'arch-angel'. In Cornwall, Wales and on the west coast of Ireland, hill-top chapels are found dedicated to St. Michael.

The tradition of St. Michael as saviour, judge of the dead and weigher of souls at the Last Judgement, current in the Middle Ages, comes from the story in Revelation of his over-coming the dragon. But it also sprang from more ancient roots, for in the Coptic period of Christianity in Egypt, the monks, continuing their indigenous worship of Osiris as judge of the dead, identified him with the sun and built chapels to him high in their monasteries, from where the rising sun could be seen. Thus, with the infiltration of the monastic tradition into the Celtic areas of the British Isles, similar high places were built; and later the tradition was carried further in the dedication of a chapel or a room high in a church.

St. Michael is depicted with flaming winged feathers, sym-bolising his status of archangel and his association with the sun; he carries a sword representing his power over evil, or scales indicating his role of weigher of truth after death. His name, 'he who is like the Lord', indicates the deepest part of a human being, the Self, which has the power to cut through error – the dragon killed by the sword of truth. It is the Self that is called upon to affirm itself at the time of the St. Michael festival at the beginning of autumn, because it is then that man's spirit could die along with nature, and he has to draw from his own resources, his awareness of I, in order to realise the birth process of Christmas.

Angel Choir, Lincoln   *Michael with scales*

MINISCULE

French, from Latin *minisculus*, 'rather small', a diminutive of *minus*, 'less'. A small letter in ancient manuscripts and also found on monuments, as opposed to a majuscule or capital. The early Christian sepulchral monuments of Ireland contained Ogham writing or a debased form of Latin capitals, or both, but from the 7th century to Norman times Latin capitals gave way to a form of writing consisting of few strokes but not yet cursive (that is, running together). About 300 examples of this miniscule writing on monuments occur in the British Isles, most of which are in Ireland and Wales. They often contain the words 'a prayer for' and the name of the deceased, and are decorated by Celtic spiral interlacing motifs.

tanto melior angelis effectus quanto

MINISTER

Latin *minister*, 'servant', as opposed to *magister*, 'master'. Someone who carries out a superior's orders or ministers to someone's needs. In the church, one who does service for the Church.

MINSTER

Greek *monastēs*, 'living alone'. (Refer to the heading 'monastery'.) The word was used in medieval times (Old English *mynster*) to designate only the church of an abbey or monastery, and now applies to churches that formerly filled that capacity. It is more loosely used to denote some of the larger cathedrals.

MISERICORD also loosely MISERERE

Latin *misericordia*, 'mercy, compassion', *misereri*, 'to have pity', *miser*, 'wretched', and *cor*, 'heart'. There are two uses of the word, both of which imply mercy by virtue of a relaxation of the monastic rule.

The most commonly understood meaning is that of the bracket or ledge on the underside of hinged seats in the choir of a cathedral, important since they represent the finest level of wood craftsmanship of the medieval period. (See under 'stalls'.) They are so called because they afforded the monks partial relief from standing during long services.

The second use is that of a room in a monastery which had some connection with the infirmary: its name varied a good deal. It was a room where indulgences were allowed, as for example the eating of meat – presumably for ill or elderly monks.

MISSAL

Ecclesiastical Latin *missale*, from *missa*, 'Mass'. A book containing the words sung and spoken in the Mass for a whole year, and describing the ritual actions performed. (See mass'.)

MITRE

Latin *mitra*, 'cap, turban', Greek *mitra*, 'belt, head-band, fillet'. Its origin is obscure however and it is more possibly connected with *Mithras*, 'god of light', from an Old Persian word. In this context, the mitre would be one of the Mithraic vestments absorbed by Christianity in Rome, as the Mithraic chief priest known as the Papa became the Christian Pope. The mitre is the official head-dress of a bishop, and starting out modestly with low sides it developed in the 13th century into a high conical cap divided by a cleft, and having two fillets or threads hanging from the back. It is likely that it assumed the shape of a fish-head with reference to Christ who was known to early Christians as the Great Fish (see 'fish').

By the 14th century the mitre had increased in size to a foot or more, and was similarly more opulent. It is recorded that one of the silver-gilt mitres from Fountains Abbey, appropriated by Henry VIII, weighed 70 ounces.

MONASTERY

Latin *monasterium*, Greek *monasterion*, 'living alone'. Greek *monazein* is 'to live alone'. The word monk is from the same root.

The beginnings of monastic life go back to the 3rd and 4th centuries, to the wandering recluses, anchorites or hermits of Egypt, as for example Ammon and Anthony. Basil who lived in the 4th century first set up rules for the purpose of the organisation of monks living together. When living together they became known as 'coenobites' (Greek *koino*, 'common' and *bios*, 'life'), and when in seclusion as 'eremites', a version of 'hermit' (Greek *erēmos*, 'solitary'). To the Church at Rome they were known as anchorites (Greek *anakhoreo*, 'I retire, withdraw'): having retired from life they had no office.

The thread appears to go through Gaul to Britain with customs and buildings necessarily undergoing modification through climate. Monastic life is first found in Bangor. Wales it should be remembered was a Druidic centre of learning which absorbed this early form of Christianity because of the connection in kind. Thence it was carried to Ireland by Patrick. Ireland remained the centre of learning until Aidan was sent to Northumbria in 635 to evangelise England. Evidence still remains of the Irish monastics in the form of beehive settlements and oratories on the west coast, and their influence is clearly seen in the early buildings at Jarrow and Wiermouth. The great monasteries of Iona, Lindisfarne and Whitby all belong to this period.

There was always variance however between the disciplinary requirements of Rome and the individual Anglo-Saxon church with its Irish monastic influence, and when Theodore was appointed to the see of Canterbury in 670 with the express purpose of introducing more conformity to rule, the spirit of monasticism in the early sense of the word could be said to have met its doom.

The Dark Ages followed, when almost all monastic buildings were destroyed by the invading Norsemen; and this was followed by the resurgence of monastic building after the Conquest in 1066. The intense religious zeal of the time produced the monastic houses of Durham, Canterbury, Norwich, Peterborough, and these, having the monopoly of learning, paved the way for the great period of cathedral building. The different monastic orders were the Benedictine, Cluniac, Cistercian, Augustinian, Premonstratensian, Carthusian, Knights Templars and Knights Hospitallers, along with the Friars and the Jesuits.

Architecturally, the church was the focus from which all sprang. The cloister adjoining in the south was surrounded by the most important buildings – refectory, chapter house, dormitory, along with the warming house, library and parlour. The infirmary and guest house and other lodgings were further removed.

MONK

Latin *monachus*, 'monk', Greek *monachos*, 'living alone'. Originally one living in solitude, performing religious exercises as in a cell or a desert. Only later did it come to imply a solitary life within a community, under vows and obeying rules of an order. (See 'monastery'.)

MONOGRAM (and other names of Christ)

Greek *monos*, 'alone, single', and *gramma*, 'something written, a letter'. Hence a joining of two or more letters to form a single significant device. The first two letters of the Greek word for Christ X and P form the monogram as in the diagram: it is sometimes called the chi-rho monogram, the sound in English of these two capitals, and this is universally used from the 4th century.

It has several variations, as the two in the diagram, sometimes being found as an X with an I (I being the initial letter of ιηcoυc, Greek for Jesus). In each case, the monogram can be seen as a six-pointed star, signifying the Logos, or Wheel of Being, a glyph where the two interlaced triangles represent the Spoken Word. Here the male triangle, base uppermost, enters and works within the substantial world, base below.

Other common abbreviations of the name of Christ can be noted under this heading. In Greek art, the cross is accompanied by the inscription ιc xc νικα or simply ιc xc. Greek C sounds 's': thus they are the first and last letters of 'ιηcoυc xpιcτoc (Jesus Christ). νικα means 'conquers' – thus 'Jesus Christ conquers'. This is sometimes abbreviated to xp νι 'Christ conquers'. In the Latin from the 12th century, Christ is designated by letters I.H.S. abbreviated from Iesus, Hominum Salvator, 'Jesus, Saviour of men'. Or in the Greek again we find IHC abbreviated from ιηcoυc, 'Jesus' or IHC with XPC, abbreviated from xpιcτoc, 'Christ' – thus 'Jesus Christ'.

The scroll found over the crucifix bears the letters INRI, an abbreviation of Iesus Nazarenus Rex Iudeorum (Jesus of Nazareth King of the Jews), though an inner symbolism gives either of two alternatives: IN NOBIS REGNAT IESUS – 'within ourselves reigns Jesus', a reference to the quest for the Christ within, and IGNE NATURA RENOVATUR INTEGRA – 'all nature is regenerated by fire', referring to the fire of the spirit regenerating the sensually orientated man.

MONSTRANCE

Old French, from Low Latin *monstrantia*, from Latin *monstrare*, 'to show'. The monstrance is the receptacle in which the consecrated Host is exposed to the congregation for adoration. This was a late ritual – circa 1300. To be visible, the host was placed in crystal, and originally many different forms were used. After the 17th century the monstrance assumed the form of the sun radiating light. Symbolically, at the moment of showing, the body has been flooded by the intelligence and life-force of the sun, dispelling darkness and error.

MONUMENT

Latin *monumentum*, 'that which calls to mind', from *monere*, 'to remind, warn', both from the same base as Latin *mens*, 'mind, reason'. Thus a tablet or tombstone or construction to the memory of someone deceased.

After the Reformation, the simple religious symbols of the Catholic faith were supplanted in the church building by more worldly emblems, Large monuments showed the mourning families of the deceased, with emblems of death and the finity of human life – skulls, crossed bones, scythe and hour-glass: later in the 17th and 18th centuries, with classical influences, came the urn, sarcophagus and pyramid. All showed a self-satisfied assurance with the inevitable frailty of human life and the blissful life to come, represented by cherubim or angels playing trumpets. The inscriptions of these times stress human concerns rather than the mystery of the inner life, and extol piety and the philanthropic acts of the deceased.

Onwards from the end of the 18th century, a sentimental element enters the scene: Faith, Hope and Charity, for example, are represented with urns and dying flowers. This is the Neo-Classical style, faithfully copying classical models. In the 19th century, monumental work was largely consigned to the graveyard outside the church.

MOON

See under 'sun and moon'.

MOULDING

Old French *molle*, *modle*, Latin *modulus*, 'a small measure': 'model' is from this root. Reference is to the cavity into which a malleable material is poured, making a pattern of the same design for a moulding – that is the narrow decorated strip of stone or wood or plaster for cornices and panelling classically, and for the decorated arches and doorways of churches later. Two well known classical moulds are the 'dentil' and the 'egg and dart' (q.v.).

Early Norman moulding is crude, but, by 1150 or so, many were in use, such as the 'chevron', 'lozenge', 'billet', 'beak-head'. Later moulding became more varied and incorporated figures, beasts, birds and flowers.

MULLION or MUNNION

Old French *moignon*, 'stump of a tree'. A mullion is the upright stone dividing the lights (the panes of the windows) and screens in Gothic architecture. They are not found prior to Early English style – in Norman work the division of the window is a shaft too heavy to be called a mullion.

MUSIC

(See under 'organ'.)

MYSTERY PLAY

The medieval dramas performed at one time in the church or church-yard, and later in the towns, presented scenes from the Bible, and were so called because they dealt with the 'mysteries' of religion. But because they were enacted by different craft guilds, an etymological complication arose. Old French for trade is *mestier* (modern French *métier*), from Latin *minister*, 'servant', giving Middle English *mistere*, mistery, 'trade or occupation'. In this sense it is claimed the dramas are 'trade dramas', literally mystery plays. However, French *mystère* is used for such dramas, and this derives from Latin *mysterium*, Greek *mustērion*, to do with initiation into religious mysteries. This is also claimed to be the true origin of the word 'mystery' in mystery play, and much 'play' has been made over the two meanings.

Like so many words, however, the two meanings are not entirely unrelated, and in this instance attention is called to the true nature of craft. A craft involves the control of matter, and since matter is only the other face of spirit, such a control may lead into the secrets of spirit: the more a man searches into the laws of a given substance, the more he is rewarded by its inherent wisdom, and a craftsman's aim is to find them and hold them and himself in a fine balance. The condition of this balance, and of true art, is love for the material being used and the subjugation of the individual will: then those perfect laws may be of service. It is for this reason that in ancient civilisations master craftsmen were held in such esteem, that they were always associated with the temple, and that the guilds continued to be quasi-religious institutions in medieval times. All that was made then was made 'to the glory of God'.

The ultimate representative of this tradition is the mason shaping the temple itself, through control of material, which had become so sensitive as to produce the delicately balanced Gothic cathedral. On the inner level, every man is a mason, shaping his own substance so that its divine origin may reveal itself to him.

Historically, the mystery play gained a hold in this country during the 13th century, superseding the 'miracle plays', distinguished by being performed by professionals. As opposed to the individual miracle plays, mystery plays were written in groups or cycles embracing a number of themes from the Old and New Testaments. Performed as part of the observation of the feast of Corpus Christi instituted in 1264, they continued as an integral part of Church life for over two hundred years. Of the many cycles only those from Chester, Coventry, Wakefield and York remain in anything like a complete state. (See 'mason' and 'freemason').

N

NARTHEX

Greek *narthex*, 'the giant fennel' or 'small casket' for unguents) from a Sanskrit root meaning 'reed'.

In the early basilica form of the early church the narthex was a long arcaded porch suggestive of the hollow stem of the plant, at the west end of the church. It was a place, like the 'galilee porch' of later years, for penitents, women or catechumens – that is those not admissible to the body of the church. Narthex is still used to denote the porch at the west end of the Catholic church containing the stoup of holy water.

Like so many other parts of the west end, the narthex has associations with the waters of life. See 'galilee', 'stoup', 'font', 'nave', 'west end'.

Latin *nativitas*, 'birth'. The Nativity, or Birth of Christ, is the first major event in the Christian calendar, leading to the Death and Resurrection. Like the Crucifixion and the Last Supper, it is often represented in iconography. On the highest level the birth is that of God on earth at the darkest point in man's involution. It is a momentous event redeeming error through the impetus of a message of love and of total surrender of the individual to the divine will. Man's darkest point is the point of the strongest concentration of his ego, and it is this that has to be surrendered. With such a birth already rooted in mankind, its effect is destined, by degrees, to transform the physical body, feeling, thinking, and the will.

In each man, the birth is of the Christ within, the new man, and this is only possible after deep anguish and darkness of the soul. In the nativity myth, the darkness is represented by the birth taking place at the sun's lowest ebb, when it would appear that the light and life of the sun is disappearing for ever. In fact Christmas is celebrated on the 25th of December when it is indisputably clear that the sun is beginning to arise in the heavens again.

The humility required for the birth to take place is symbolised by the stable – both the ox and ass are beasts of burden. The birth of the child, the original Christmas present, is of a virgin, indicating that it can only take place within the purity of the soul. Again, it is simple shepherds who bear the good tidings; and all aspects of the story affirm the need to return to innocence. (See 'Magi' for further symbolism.)

Latin *navis*, 'ship'. The nave in the church is the place of the people, the place where the people are saved. The ship is the Church of Christ which upholds the souls of men above the storms of the waters of materiality.

On a larger scale, spiritual truths are protected in this ship or ark through periodic deluges. Truth may be submerged by ignorance, but the ark contains the seed of its future rebirth. The same ark is seen in the cradle which upheld Moses and saved him and the Jews from the forces of oppression symbolised by Pharoah. And in a way, each individual human being is born into the waters of life, where he is cut adrift at the *navel*, the source of physical succour, and where he must find his own salvation in the spiritual ship.

Latin *nimbus* 'cloud, thunder-cloud'. The word in Christian art came to mean the bright vaporous light around the head of a divine being. It is of pagan origin, the Romans using it as an indication of the power of the sun around the head of celebrated mortals, but, in Christian art after the 11th century, it was reserved exclusively for saints, martyrs, apostles and for Christ himself. There are many variations of shape, including the ring, disc, triangle and square. Other names for the nimbus are 'halo' and inaccurately 'aureole' and 'glory' (q.v.). Latin *nimbus* however is a materialistic image for the light is that inner radiance which comes of spiritual purity.

The cruciform nimbus, one of the most common in all Christian art, is exclusively reserved for Deity and especially for the Son, the Second Person of the Trinity, referring to Christ's sacrifice as man on the cross. Representations of Christ without it are rare. (See 'halo'.)

NINE ALTARS

In the retro-choir of some cathedrals are the Chapels of the Nine Altars, connected with the nine orders of angels in Church doctrine. (See 'angel'.)

Symbolically it could be said that between God and man, or between man realising his own divinity, lie nine levels. 9 is the square of 3, the Trinity, representing the unfolding of these divine powers in body, heart and mind. It is a magical number, complete in the sense of non-changing – for instance 9 plus 9 equals 18, and the sum of the digits 1 and 8 make 9. Equally 9 times 9 is 81 and the sum of these digits makes 9. The end of the ninth month in the womb gives way to a new birth, as the expiration of the ninth hour on the Cross rent the veil into the eternal plane.

NOAH

Noah is a Hebrew word meaning 'rest'. Noah and the ark riding the flood is one of the most commonly depicted themes in the Church. As a church is a ship of salvation in the waters of materiality (see under 'nave'), so the ark is a vessel, if we extend the imagery to cosmic cycles, which saves Truth from being submerged by error. The allegory says that man's wickedness may bring about his own destruction, but each new cycle has in it the pure eternal seed that allows the continued growth of the spirit and the fulfilling of man's ultimate purpose on earth. Thus Noah represents both the rest between such cycles and the Divine Intelligence, Greek *Nous*, that oversees this development.

His three sons represent the three parts of man's being, the three natural divisions of consciousness – head, heart and will. *Japhet* means 'the extender', a word used in connection with the northern portions of the world as then known (head); *Shem* means 'name, fame', in the sense of the 'name of God', God as love (heart); and *Ham* is a word originally meaning Egypt, derived from an Egyptian word *kem*, 'black' (will). The animals, clean and unclean, represent all that has gone before, external and internal to man's development, which is being carried through to the next cycle. God's grace and forgiveness – indicated in the story by the dove and the olive leaf, both symbols of love and reconciliation of heaven and earth – is also symbolised by the rainbow. The continuing overseership of the Divine Intelligence in the new cycle is symbolised by the high mountain Ararat where the ark finally comes to rest.

NORBERTINES

A monastic order. See under the alternative name 'Premonstratensian'.

NORMAN

Old French *Normant*, 'North-man', describing the Scandinavian race who conquered Normandy in the 10th century and settled there. This Norman/French race conquered England in 1066, bringing with them an unprecedented spate of building in which the churches of the religious orders and most parish churches were built. The Anglo-Saxon features were replaced by the apse, central tower, the three storeys of the basilica, and a western doorway. The cathedrals and abbey churches emphatically showed this Norman style, but it was not long before the indigenous English tradition reasserted itself. By the 13th century, most east ends were pulled down giving place to the square end and greater height. The central tower however remained the most distinctive feature of English cathedrals and abbeys. Among the many features are arched windows and decorated arched doorways.

Norman

NUN

Middle English *nunne*, *nonne*, from Low Latin *nunna*, *nonna*, meaning 'old lady'. The meaning has come through Greek *nenna*, *nannē*, 'aunt and uncle': and all from Sanskrit *nanā*, 'mother'. In medieval times the word was used as a term of respect for a woman of age and experience, especially that of motherhood; in the same way an old man was respected in the term *nonnus*. Thus it is respect and veneration for experience that is found in the use of the word when it came to be applied to a woman belonging to a religious order.

O

OGEE

Old French *augive*, meaning a 'double curved arch'. Further than that, the origin of the word is doubtful. In this form of arch, the line of each side is composed of a concave and a convex curve. The single line of such an arch also constitutes a form of moulding known as ogee.

OGHAM

Old Irish *ogum*, modified to *ogham*, from the name of the legendary Ogna. A Celtic system of writing (British and

Irish) consisting of twenty letters formed by short strokes made at either side of a transverse line, usually at the angle of the tall stones upon which the writing is found. They are mostly sepulchral stones bearing the names of the deceased and his father, usually joined by a word equivalent to the Scottish 'mac'. The writing is often found along with debased capitals, and several have crosses showing the joining of Celtic and Christian cultures.

OIL

Latin *oleum*, Greek *elaion*, 'olive-oil'. Oil is symbolically 'love' – the power of compassion. Oil burns, illuminating by its light, the light of Wisdom: externally and internally it is a lubricant and makes for the smooth inter-relating of parts, as its psychological counterpart, love, makes for unity between men. It is love that leads to Wisdom. (See in more detail, variously, under 'Christ', 'candle', 'unction'.)

ORATORY

From Latin *oratorium*, from *orator*, 'one who speaks or prays'. A chapel for private prayer. In current usage, the oratory is a building often attached to a church for private prayer, or a chapel for private or family worship in a stately home.

The name originated in the early Christian Church. In the 5th and 6th centuries, Irish monks inhabited beehive huts, the continuation of a pagan style, and performed devotions in an adjacent building called an oratory. The oratory differed from the hut simply in that it had a raised platform acting as an altar and a rectangular ground plan taking sloping walls to a roof angle.

Later Continental influence brought the chancel and the bell-tower. But the art of masonry continued. Stone roofs meant small churches and so there was the early practice of not enlarging a church but building other churches on the site; this continued up to medieval times and gives the typically Irish feature of a group of small churches around the original oratory of the founder saint.

ORB

Latin *orbis*, 'ring, circle'. In Christian art, an orb is a globe surmounted by a cross, frequently depicted held by Christ as a child, and also in images of God the Creator. The cross symbolises the power of Christ's Crucifixion over the orb or circle of confinement which is the world. (See 'cross' and 'five wounds'.)

ORDER

Middle English *ordre*, from Latin *ordo*, 'a regular series, or arrangement': also 'a class or rank', as in a monastic fraternity. The order in architecture refers to the styles in Greek architecture, basically three in number – Doric, Ionian and Corinthian (q.v.) – though the Romans in resurrecting these orders added two others, Tuscan and Composite. The order embraces the whole base, shaft, capital and entablature. (See 'column' and 'capital'.)

ORGAN

Latin *organum*, 'instrument, tool', Greek *organon*, 'instrument, tool': related to Greek *ergon*, 'work, energy'. Only in medieval times did the word come to be used specifically for the musical instrument, the organ.

It is strange how the word came into use. Clearly the musical 'organum' of medieval times, a system of singing in intervals of 4ths and 5ths, and the organ itself, are related, and that both are in some sense a tool. Music making, this suggests, is a tool in the hands of man – essentially an aspiring and yearning of the spirit. Organ and organum are both then instrumental in linking man with God.

The need for harmony in the soul is also implied; inner work is to do with achieving harmony. Harmony in music has a scientific basis, for the most pleasing and perfect intervals have the most simple mathematical ratios – e.g. the octave has 1-2, the fifth 2-3, the fourth 3-4 and so on: it was only these elementary intervals that organum originally employed. Spatial harmony was also understood by the master builders of the cathedrals; relationship of transept to the whole length of the church, length to width of transept and so on, are known to have been considered in the light of the most simple ratios. Thus there was a subtle resonance between the harmony of the music and the harmony of the space it filled.

Historically, portable machines of the organ family were used in Graeco-Roman times, mostly in places of entertainment. The Church may not have accepted the instrument at first because of its secular association – certainly there is little reference to the 'organ' in the first few centuries of Christianity. In the 10th century, however, there are references to organs in Britain, along with indications of their laborious size and the manpower needed to supply air to the bellows. Organs were not used in ordinary parish churches, and here, music was the responsibility of wind and string instrumentalists, who prior to the Reformation played in the broad rood loft in front of the chancel, and later in a gallery at the west end of the church. There is always evidence in the internal structure of a church of the difficulty found in accomodating the organ or harmonium when they began to supplant live musicians in the 19th century.

ORIEL WINDOW or ORIOLE

Medieval Latin *oriolum*, 'recess, gallery', probably from Latin *oratoriolum*, a diminutive of *oratorium*, 'place of prayer'. Originally it was part of a house set apart for prayer in medieval times. From such a place, the lord of the house could look down upon and participate in a domestic service. Any projecting room, private chamber or gallery came to be called an oriole, still with its religious function; and finally the term came to mean simply a projecting window, either corbelled high up on a wall or rising straight from ground level.

OVOLO

Latin *ovum*, 'egg'. A classical and Renaissance convex moulding, usually a quarter of a circle, and often decorated by an egg and dart motif.

P

PALIMPSEST

A Latin word from Greek *palimpsēston*, from *palin*, 'again'; 'in reverse direction' and *psaio*, 'rub, crumble away'. The term refers to parchment upon which two sets of writings are found superimposed, and also to church brasses where the brass has been used on the other side for engraving, or over-engraving by changing the existing design. It was a common occurrence in the days of early manuscripts to re-use old parchment from which the writing had been erased, and often an older and more valuable document has been uncovered by careful deciphering of the original.

Latin *pallium*, 'cloak', and *palla*, 'woman's outer garment'. Thus the idea of a covering in the current meanings of either a small square of linen laid over the chalice or the black-purple cloth covering a coffin.

The word pall has a deep significance: it is essentially the cover upon God's own power by the act of creation. Its blackness is the heaviness of gravity and the *maya* that ensnares man's spirit. The word 'pale' gives a similar image of loss of life, and the verb 'to pall' suggests becoming weary by excess, especially of sensual indulgence. The whole idea is reflected in the associated word 'fall', as in the sense of the fall of man. To be appalled is to be aware of the truth of the situation.

PANTRY

Medieval Latin *panetaria*, 'bread-shop' (*panis*, 'bread'). A room in a monastery in which the bread and table necessities were kept. The buttery or botellerie (French *bouteille*, 'bottle'), as distinct from the pantry, contained all wines, beer and drinking utensils.

PARADISE

See under 'parvis' and in the context of the Garden of Eden under that heading.

PARCLOSE

Old French *parclos*, past participle of *parclore*, 'to shut in' (*per* and *clore* 'to close'). A parclose is a screen or railing in a church which encloses a shrine or tomb or shuts off a side chapel from the main body of the church.

PARISH AND PARISH CHURCH

Latin *paroecia*, 'parish', Greek *paroikia*, 'land around a church' – *para*, 'beside' and *oiein*, 'to dwell'. Thus a parish is originally the smallest area in the jurisdiction of a rector or vicar, a division of a diocese.

Most parish churches in Britain had their origin in the Norman period and were of simple form, with or without transepts. With few exceptions they underwent many changes and present a confusing picture to the observer. The east end seems to be the first to have undergone enlargement. Later, as more accommodation was needed, aisles were added (most churches had none). Of the two aisles, the north aisle was

added first due to the south side of the churchyard being preferred as a burial ground. In such an instance, the nave wall
was often pierced leaving the upper part sustained by later
pillars. Aisles were often added to both nave and chancel.

Later, aisles were again widened so that the aisle roof was
brought level with the eaves of the nave roof, and in larger
churches this meant the covering over of the clerestory; traces
of this change can be seen on nave walls. At the chancel end,
chantry chapels were often built on both north and south sides,
so widening the whole church. Again, transepts would be
widened to compensate for other changes. In the 14th century,
a nave and chancel were seen more as a unit, and chancel
arches were enlarged, but the overriding change was in the
development of the rood-screen, which replaced the chancel
arch, and became the characteristic of the medieval church.
These in turn were in the main destroyed at the Reformation,
causing visible structural changes. Thus many parish churches,
in their architecture and fittings, represent almost a millenium
of history, not counting a possible prior Saxon origin.

PARLOUR

Old French, *parleor*, from Latin *parlare*, 'to talk'. The
parlour is a small room found in monasteries where talking
was permitted, as for instance on the subject of trade, and
private matters needing discussion. The room was only available on the consent of the prior or abbot. It was also known
as a 'locutary'.

PARSON

Latin *persona*, 'human being, person' from the current
medieval phrase '*ecclesiae persona*', the person representing
the church in a parish. The other meaning of Latin *persona*
can be considered too – 'character, role', as on a stage, for
the representative of the Church acts out man's spiritual
drama in the rituals he performs.

PARVIS

Old French *parevis*, from Medieval Latin *paravisus*, from
Latin *paradisus*, 'paradise'. (The basic meaning of 'paradise',
deriving from Persian, is 'an enclosure or garden'.) The word
was first used in medieval times to denote the actual court-
yard in front of St. Peter's Church in Rome, and only later
came to mean the enclosed space in front of the western face
of a cathedral or church. In the early Christian Church, such

a forecourt had a fountain used for symbolic washing and for those not yet baptised. There is also the obvious imagery that paradise can be regained through entering the west door of the church.

The word is used loosely to denote the west porch of a church, and also a small room above the main west porch, looking out onto the forecourt. There is also obvious imagery in the fact that when the faithful enter the enclosure of the church they are symbolically re-entering paradise.

PASSION

Latin *passio*, 'suffering, emotion'. The Passion refers to Christ's suffering on the cross and thus means a description of the Crucifixion in the Gospels or a representation of it in art. The word 'passion' has two common emotive colourings. One suggests the suffering of Christ in his conscious role of taking the burden of man's sins by his death, an act of awful solemnity involving compassion (com-passion, 'with passion'), love and reverence for others. The other is found in the meaning of violent anger, the unruly energy of the crowd that rejects Christ.

Thus in the imagery of the crucifixion, the element of reverential awe is side by side with the ignorant passion of the crowd: and in an individual man, the capacity for true suffering, for his own state and for others, is at war with his passion, his lower nature which mocks and destroys the other.

PASTORAL STAFF

'Pastoral' is from Latin *pastor*, 'shepherd'; staff is from Middle English *staf*, Old High German *stab*, 'staff, stick'. (See 'crozier'.)

PATEN

Old French *patens*, Latin *patena*, 'pan, shallow dish', from Greek *patanē*, 'pan'. A paten is a small shallow dish, usually of gold, silver or pewter, used to hold the wafer in the celebration of the Eucharist. It is made to match a particular chalice though most of the medieval patens preserved have become separated from their chalices. When preserved together it is often due to the tradition in the 13th and 14th centuries to inter them with the ecclesiastics who used them.

PATTEE or PATEE CROSS

French *patte*, 'paw, foot'. In heraldry, a cross with the arms having a broad flat end. It is sometimes called a 'Maltese cross', but this is an error. (See 'Maltese cross'.)

PAUL

See under 'Peter and Paul'.

PAX

Latin *pax*, 'peace'. Originally, during the celebration of the Mass, the members of the congregation received the kiss of peace, the *osculum pacis*, from the priest. Later, for convenience, a small tablet of gold or silver, bearing an image of the Crucifixion, to which the priest had already given the kiss of peace, was passed around to be kissed by the congregation.

PECTORAL CROSS

Latin *pectus*, 'breast'. The cross is usually of solid gold or silver, bejewelled and worn on the breast by bishops and abbots, and often contains a holy relic. In its position on the breast, the cross acts as a prism for forces flowing out through the bishop into the communicant.

PEDIMENT

The word is thought to be a form of 'periment', a version of pyramid. It originally denoted the triangular structure crowning the front of a Greek building, and then came to mean any such structure, triangular or rounded, over a portico or door. A more likely origin of the word, however, is from the two parts of the word, *ped* and *ment* (Latin stems respectively, 'foot' and 'mind'): *ped* here is seen as a euphemism for sexual power.

This would point to the significance of the triangle in the Greek civilisation in relation to the unfolding of man's inner development. The foot or base of the triangle represents the material forces of gravity and the enslaved energy, and the apex of the triangle the forces of light, of Apollonian order, mental development pulling upwards. The resulting isosceles triangle represents the potential equilibrium between the two.

The pediment was known to the Greek as the *aetos*, the 'eagle', and was considered a particular gift of the gods. The space in the triangle was called the *tympanum*, 'kettle-drum', suggesting the tension between the opposing forces, and was filled with sculpture – as that of Phidias on the Parthenon. It was considered the crown of the temple in the same way that the carving over the cathedral door was considered the consummation of all artistic effort. (See 'tympanum'.)

PELICAN

Greek *pelekinos*, from *pelekys*, 'axe': originally a Babylonian-Assyrian word *pillaqu*, 'axe'. The connection with axe is found in the related Greek word *pelekas*, 'wood-pecker'.

The sacrifice or wounding theme is found in the fable of the pelican where the young were reputed to be fed by the disgorging of its own blood. Thus it came to symbolise the sacrificial act of Christ on the cross and was in early Christianity used as a symbol of Christ's life work. Examples are found carved on early lecterns in place of the now customary eagle; and the pelican is also found in heraldry. Though the feeding on the blood is now disproven, the large pouch from which food is disgorged remains an image of the nurturing of the young in spirit.

PENDANT

Latin *pendere*, 'to hang'. An ornament hanging from the ceiling, associated with the Perpendicular period, and especially found in stone vaultings, as in fan-vaulting where the fan spreads out from the pendant. They were often richly carved.

PENTAGRAM or PENTALPHA

Greek *penta*, 'five' and *gramma*, 'something written or drawn': the five-pointed star is also called a 'pentalpha' because its form appears to be the consequence of five interlocking 'a's (*alpha*, Greek 'a').

PERPENDICULAR

A period of English architecture following on from the Decorated, approximately 1377 to 1485, and broadly equated with the 15th century. It is typified by the upright lines of the bars of windows and of panelling. Larger windows necessitated transoms; that is, horizontal bars. Since the arcades of the nave and clerestory windows were heightened, the triforium was almost dispensed with. In the vaulting, complex ribs and panels give rise to the fan and pendant vaults. The style is also referred to as Rectilinear, with especial reference to window tracery.

Perpendicular

PETER AND PAUL

St. Peter and St. Paul are both establishers of the Church in Rome, and in iconography stand next to the Evangelists in importance. They are commonly represented at either side of Christ enthroned, or at either side of the altar.

Peter (Greek *petros*, 'stone' – referring to his function of founder of the Church) – holds the two crossed keys, one gold one silver, the insignia of the papacy. (For symbolic aspects of the 'key', see under that heading.) Paul (Latin *paulus*, 'small') was so named after his conversion: before this he held the Hebrew name Saul. Clearly the name Paulus would have a spiritual significance, and the literal translation itself indicates smallness, in the sense of humility and unworthiness to receive the gift of revelation. In his own words he considered himself 'less than the least of the Apostles'. Paul is represented with a sword, referring both to his martyrdom and to his warrior-like work in spreading the message of Christ. He also carries a book indicating the importance of his message, that it is a new dispensation not only for the Jews but for all men.

Old French *puie*, 'raised seat, balcony', from Latin *podium*
and Greek *podion*. The word was originally applied to a
raised place from which a preacher read, and later acquired
the meaning of a compartment or stall or fixed bench for a
congregation: the term 'pew' simply indicates that the construction was raised.

From the 14th century, the nave of larger churches had
fixed seats of oak with carved ends at the aisles, sometimes
with finials (called 'poppies'). The propertied families had
their own high, enclosed pews, sometimes called stalls, and
paid for the privilege of such pews according to their near-
ness to the altar: in fact, in smaller churches, there was little
room for the common people. In cathedrals, families of distinction, the patrons of the establishment, erected pews immediately to right and left of the altar, and some of these
edifices, made of stone, still remain. The nave however originally had no seating as such. Sometimes a stone bench is
found along the inner walls for the use of the aged and infirm, and this gave rise to the expression 'the weakest go to
the wall' or 'to go to the wall'.

In parish churches after the Commonwealth, long benches
superseded the family pew system, expressing the emancipa-
tion of the people; indications of the old high pews can be
seen in columns of the nave where pieces have been cut away.
(See 'stalls'.)

PIER

Low Latin *pera*, through Greek *petra*, 'rock'. A mass of
stone, as opposed to a column, supporting an arch or a roof.
The word is, however, loosely used instead of 'pillar' in Norman and Gothic architecture, and even sometimes in place of
'column'. A pillar has more of an ornamental character,
though fulfilling the same function as the pier.

PILASTER

From pillar (q.v.) and *aster* (a Latin suffix indicating dimi-
nution or inferiority). Thus a pilaster is a flat, rectangular
column against a wall with a shaft, distinctive base and capital, but with the base projecting only about a third of its
depth from the wall.

131

PILLAR

Latin *pila*, 'pillar', the etymology of which is said to be doubtful. A support, not necessarily of classical proportions, for an arch or roof. Whereas a column is round, a pillar may be clustered, composed of several smaller columns making a massive whole. Each period has its own particular form.

Symbolically the pillar is a sustaining power, a bridge between lower and higher levels, earth and spirit. In man the pillar is the vertical spine which raises him heavenwards out of the earth and around which lie subtle channels of energy connecting sex and head centres. A pillar of fire, in biblical reference, is the regenerated energy; a pillar of salt is the energy retained to the service of the lower self. The capital I is a glyph for that pillar with its two possible directions.

The pillar, in ancient symbolism, is dual in another way: there are two pillars, for example, in the forecourt of Solomon's Temple, indicating the hazardous nature of the opposites through which a delicate path has to be trod. Here, as elsewhere, the two pillars say that the world cannot exist without polar relationship on all levels, but that the duality must be reconciled in a fine point of balance. This is suggested in most medieval cathedrals, for there are two towers, one at either side of the west door, which when opened leads the eye in a direct line under the single central tower, to the altar, the place of final reconciliation.

The danger of the dual pillars is also suggested in comparing the Latin *pila* with *pilare*, 'to rob, deprive of hair' (*pilus*, 'hair'). Deprived of power (hair is always symbolically a man's power) he has to erect his own unifying 'pillar'.

PILGRIM

Middle English *pelegrin*, Latin *peregrinus*, 'foreign'; *per*, 'beyond' and *ager*, 'territory'. Thus someone who voyages away from home; the main purpose of foreign travel, in the days in which the word originated, was to visit a religious shrine.

PINNACLE

Low Latin *pinnaculum*; *pinna*, 'point' and *culus*, a diminutive suffix. In Gothic architecture, it is the slender turret-like point on buttresses, roofs or parapets, often decorated with foliage.

PISCINA

Latin *piscina*, 'fish-pond', from *piscis*, 'fish'. A piscina is a stone basin in a niche in the wall of a church near the altar, and sometimes in the ground near the altar, used by the priest for washing his hands before and during the celebration of the Mass and for cleansing the chalice after use. The piscina is usually found in this country on the south wall and, in the earlier periods of architecture, two may be found together.

The association with the fish is due to the special symbolism of the fish. Due to the fact of Christ's birth heralding the zodiacal era of Pisces (the Fishes), there were many uses of this symbol in early Christianity. (See 'fish'.)

PLINTH

Latin *plinthus*, 'plinth', Greek *plinthos*, 'brick'. The plinth is the lowest part of the base of a column, classically plain and square, but in Gothic columns subdivided and moulded.

POPPY-HEAD

Latin *puppis*, 'the poop of a ship'. (French *poupée*, 'doll', is so named from the carved poop). *Puppis* is connected with *papa*, 'father', both from a root meaning 'to swell'. A poppy-head is the raised and ornamented top of the ends of benches in a church, often cut in the form of a fleur-de-lis. Many can be seen in the choir stalls of cathedrals and some in the naves of parish churches. None exist prior to the 14th century, and they are associated mainly with the Perpendicular period. Another name for poppy-head is 'standard'.

PORTICO or PORCH

Latin *porticus*, 'a colonnade' or 'covered gallery', from *portus*, 'entrance, harbour'. In a large church the portico or porch is the covered entrance at the west front: it also refers to the projecting entrance in either the north or south walls.

The translation 'port' provides yet another instance of the 'water' symbolism associated with the west end of the church: the image is of the sea of life the soul enters at birth. Water is in the stoup and the font, and the nave is the ship on that sea. (See 'west end', 'east end' 'nave' for symbolism.)

133

PREACHER

Old French *prechier*, from Latin *praedicare*, 'to proclaim, announce' (*prae* 'forwards' and *dicere*, 'to speak'). Thus one who speaks forth the gospel.

PREDELLA

Italian, 'a foot-stool' or 'kneeling stool'. The origin of the word is not certain, but it is likely that the letter 'r' has intruded into the Latin root *ped*, 'foot'. It denotes a step or platform on which an altar rests; it also denotes a raised structure behind the altar itself. The raised dais for the altar is also referred to as a 'foot-pace'.

PREMONSTRATENSIANS or NORBERTINES

An Augustinian monastic order founded by St. Norbert in France in 1120. The name derives from French *pré* and *montré*, Latin *pratum monstratum*, 'the indicated meadow', because it was shown to him in a dream that he should erect his monastery at that particular place. This order was known by the name White Canons of Augustine. There were 35 houses extant in Britain at the Dissolution, of which Eastby Abbey in Yorkshire is one.

PRESBYTERY

Latin *presbyterium*, from Greek *presbutērion*, 'the place of the presbyters' (*presbuteros*, 'elder', from *presbus*, 'old').

The presbytery is thus in the eastern end of the church, in the sanctuary where the clergy perform their rituals: the term is often applied to the whole sanctuary but it is specifically the area east of the choir and before the altar. In a cathedral it is usually elevated one step above the choir and has the name 'gradus presbyterii'.

PRESBYTER

From the same root as 'presbytery'. Thus the meaning of an elder or leader in the early Church giving the word 'priest'. Later, in the Presbyterian Church, such a priest was called an 'elder'. The term 'presbyter' now also denotes a group of presbyters meeting in and representing a given district.

PRIEST

Middle English *prēst*, from Old High German *priester*, derived from the Latin *presbyter* through Greek *presbuteros*, 'elder' (*presbus*, 'old'). The original meaning from *presbus* is 'leader of a herd'; compare Latin *prae*, 'before' (Greek *para*, 'proceeding from') and Greek *bous*, 'ox'. The venerated leader of the animal kingdom became the leader in the world of the spirit.

PRIORY AND PRIOR

Old French *priorie*, from Latin *prioria*, 'former, better', from a base as in *primus* meaning 'first'. A branch monastery of nuns or monks subordinate to an abbey is called a priory. In the same way that an abbey derives its name from an abbot ('father'), the priory is so called from the prior, the first in rank under the abbot.

PULPIT

Latin *pulpitum*, 'platform, stage, scaffold'. The pulpit is the raised structure from which the minister addresses the congregation. Formerly such platforms, made of stone or wood, were attached to a wall or pillar in the nave for the address to the congregation. Very few pulpits remain of earlier date than the Perpendicular period, and these are polygonal in shape and often approached by a concealed stairway: they frequently have finely ornamented canopies. Pulpits were also erected in the refectories of monasteries for readings at meals.

In the sense that the priest is a vehicle for divine prophecy, for the power of God, the pulpit is properly on his right side – to the left of the chancel as seen by the congregation. The lectern containing the Book, the formulated Word, is on the opposite side. (See 'right and left'.)

PULPITUM

(Same derivation as 'pulpit'.) The term 'pulpitum' is sometimes used instead of 'rood-loft' (see 'rood'), the screen with gallery above, supporting the great crucifix and separating the nave from the chancel in pre-Reformation times. It was also the high place from which readings were made. In cathedrals, such a stone screen with gallery, often housing the organ, is invariably a 'pulpitum'. It usually contains statues of saints or kings and intricate canopy work. This sculpture suffered much at the Reformation and was subject to much restoration later.

PURBECK MARBLE

A type of marble from Purbeck in Dorset used for columns in some of the early cathedrals, and giving a highly polished finish. In later centuries, the marble was much used for the making of memorials and tombs.

PYX

Latin *pyxis*, Greek *pyxis*, 'a box'. (Greek *pyxos*, the 'box-tree, boxwood'). A pyx is a casket containing the Host (the wafer symbolising the sacrificed body of Christ). It is used in the blessing of the people in certain services, and also for carrying to the sick. In classical times, it was simply a box in which valuables were kept, but Christianity adopted it as a receptacle for relics and for the reserved sacrament. The pyx and the ciborium (q.v.) were both used for this purpose, but latterly the ciborium was a larger vessel for use on the altar, and the pyx, smaller, came to be used for administering the Host to the dying (the viaticum).

Q

QUARREL

Old French *quarrel*, from Medieval Latin *quadrellus*, diminutive of Latin *quadrus*, 'a square'. A small square diamond, or square-shaped pane of glass, fitted by lead into a window: also an opening of four leaves in tracery of the Perpendicular period.

QUATREFOIL

See under 'trefoil'.

QUIRE

See under 'choir'.

QUOIN

Old French *coign* and Modern French *coin*, 'corner', from Latin *cuneus*, 'wedge'. In Saxon architecture especially, it denotes the angle of a church wall where the wall is of rough stonework and the corner or quoin is of dressed stone. The name is also used to denote the individual stones of which the whole quoin is built.

R

RAGULY CROSS

Middle English *ragge*, Old Norwegian *rogg*, 'tuft of fur or rough hair'. Thus a cross whose limbs are notched at equal distances on both sides.

REBUS

Latin *rebus*, the ablative plural of *res*, 'thing, object'. An enigmatical representation of a name, by pictures suggesting parts of the name, in the nature of a riddle. Such a device is found in coats-of-arms, quite apart from heraldry, and on monuments and tombs. Members of the clergy especially were subject to such treatment.

RECTOR

Latin *rector*, 'leader, ruler', a word applied in Low Latin to a bishop, abbot or priest. In the English Church he was an incumbent, a parish priest who had the right to the greater tithes of corn, wood and hay, as well as to the lesser tithes. This privilege, as well as the freehold of the rectory, continues today despite the effects of the Dissolution of the Monasteries, when many rectorial tithes came to an end, some being sold to non-ecclesiastics who were called 'lay-rectors'. A vicar (q.v.) does not have this protection.

REFECTORY

Latin *refectio*, 'a re-making, re-freshment', from *reficere*, 'to re-make' – thus the general idea of restoring the body through food. The dining hall of a monastery was usually on the south side of the cloister. The terms FRATER, FRATERY, FRATRY, from an old French abbreviation *fraitur*, are also used. When erected over the vaulted cellars and above ground level, the refectory is referred to as a FRATER OVER.

REFORMATION

Literally, a re-formation of the state of religion, it was a long tradition of dissatisfaction and protest (hence Protestantism) expressed mainly against papal rule, both spiritual and temporal. The leaders were Wycliffe (1324-84), Luther (1483-1546), Zwingli (1484-1531), Calvin (1509-64), and Knox (1513-72). Behind the English Reformation lay the attempt of

Henry VIII to extend the power of the monarchy into all aspects of national life. This came to a head in the controversies of the early 16th century with the Suppression of the Monasteries (q.v.), and culminated in the Act of Supremacy of 1559 during the reign of Elizabeth.

In terms of the church interior, this involved drastic changes. All images connected with the Roman Creed were destroyed or defaced. What was enforced by Edward VI was applied even more rigorously under Elizabeth, so that not only the wooden roods and rood-screens (q.v.) were destroyed, but also paintings on walls.

The Reformation was however an inevitable move away from medieval innocence to sophistication through knowledge, and the growth of a sense of individual importance. Such a change involved the throwing off of the yoke of the Roman Church, and this was encouraged by the spirit of the Renaissance which filtered into this country during the reign of Henry VIII. Medieval building and tradition was dying; enough churches had been produced in the medieval period and so it was not in new churches, but in the interiors of the old, that changes were henceforth made. There was now a deterioration in style – the humanity of the new grew into a visible complacency, most noticeable in the expressions of the wealthy donors on memorial monuments. On tombs, records of the worldly attainments of the deceased were preferred to sacred figures. Many factors were involved: Flemish craftsmen had already brought classical idioms into Henry's court, and the massacre of St. Bartholomew later gave rise to the influx of Huguenot craftsmen. Literature, printing, the introduction of a book of Common Prayer, and classical ideals – all contributed to this flowering of a new age.

RELIC AND RELIQUARY

Middle English *relyke* from Latin *reliquiae*, 'remains'. Thus, some part of the body of a martyr or saint kept for religious veneration. Originally bones were the principal relics, but later the intimate possessions of a saint were kept for the same purpose. For example, in Ireland in the 5th and 6th centuries, the bible, bell and crozier (pastoral staff) belonging to the founder of a particular church were treasured as having magical properties, and each article had its own custodian. Metal covers called reliquaries or shrines were made to cover them, and these give us some of the finest Celtic art of the time.

RENAISSANCE

French, literally *re-naissance*, 're-birth': specifically the re-birth of ancient Greek ideals, art and literature during the 15th and 16th centuries in Europe. (The original Italian word was similarly *rinascita*, 're-birth'.) Formerly only describing a change in style, it was only in the 19th century that it came to signify a whole period. Exact dates are not easily definable. Petrarch in the 14th century had already started a return to classical Roman forms, and Florentine artists developed this revival.

The transplanting of the Gothic spiritual aspiration, with its quality of primitive innocence, into the new growth of naturalism was an inevitable step in the individualising of man. The movement out into the world of scientific clarity was a move from the nameless work of Gothic craftsmen to the birth of an individual self-awareness which, whilst extolling the virtues of man, was destined to end in a stale imitation of the original.

The influence from Italy passed into northern Europe at different times, until finally no aspect of Western life, including thought, language, music, science and medicine, remained untouched by it. In England, though Henry VIII had employed Italian workmen earlier, it was only in the 17th century that Inigo Jones introduced the true Renaissance idiom. Prior to this so-called Tudor Gothic style, the heavy Jacobean style between 1600 and 1625 had already moved away from pure Gothic. Wren, in the 17th century, broke new ground in building his London churches, for there had been no previous model for churches classically designed, and his ingenuity produced many variants of roof, column and steeple. (See 'column' and 'order'.)

REREDORTER

Rere and *dorter*, from Old French *arere*, 'at the back', and *dorter*, an abbreviation of the word 'dormitory' (Latin *dormire*, 'to sleep'). Thus the reredorter is the room at the back of the dormitory containing closets and having wooden seats, divided partitions, and a drain of flowing water.

REREDOS

Old French, *arere* means 'at the back', and *dos* is from Latin *dorsum*, 'back'. The reredos is the screen at the back of the altar, often highly ornamented with carving. They vary in height – some, for example the one in Durham cathedral, rising almost to the roof.

RESPOND

Latin *respondere*, 'to reply'. Half of a pillar or a pier projecting from a wall to support an arch, as at the chancel: thus the idea of one part of the arch responding to, or meeting, the other.

RESURRECTION

Latin *resurrectionem*, 'rising from the dead', from the past participle *resurrectum* or *resurgere*, 'to rise again, re-surge'. The actual Resurrection of Christ is not described in the Gospels, and representations of the rising from the tomb do not appear until the 13th century. Usually, the three Marys were shown at an empty sepulchre. Representations became increasingly literal and humanised, contributing to the erroneous thinking of the resurrected body as the ultimate and fixed state of man after death. The Resurrection symbolises a new and re-righted spiritual state in a man, following upon total surrender of the self. It also indicates that there is a potential new relationship with the physical body, which allows it to be used not for itself but for purposes of the spirit. Finally it indicates, along with the ascension, certain natural changes in states of consciousness.

RETABLE

Latin, *re*, 'back', and table. A shelf or ledge found behind and above the altar, holding the cross and other miscellaneous vases.

RETRO-CHOIR

Latin *retro*, 'at the back, behind', and choir: thus the part of the church behind the place where choir sits. It is usually in the form of an ambulatory or walking place behind the high altar.

RETURNED STALLS

Stalls in the choir of a cathedral are so named when they turn transversely from their general east to west direction, at their western end. Such stalls are allotted to dignitaries, and many have intricate canopy work, one of the features of the cathedral. Many however suffered in the name of restoration.

RIB VAULTING

A projecting band which ornaments, or is part of the structure, of a ceiling. Plain ribs crossing at right-angles in Norman work gave way to intersecting ribs. In the English periods, groins have ribs (groins are the intersecting edges formed by vaults meeting), and intersecting ribs have bosses. During the latter part of the 14th and 15th centuries, the increase in the number of ribs brought about 'fan vaulting' where the ribs start individual drop points (pendentives) and become functional arches. (See 'lierne vaulting').

RIB AND PANEL VAULTING

This vaulting supplanted the Norman type where individual vaults crossed, forming groins (see the above entry). The ribs supported thin stone panels.

RIGHT AND LEFT

'Right' is from Old High German *reht*, cognate with Latin *rectus*, 'right, straight', and Greek *erektos*, 'erect'. 'Left' is from Middle English *lift* or *left*, originally meaning 'weak, infirm'. Old English is *lēf*, 'infirm, diseased', and derives from Latin *letum*, 'death'.

Right, and all its associated meanings, are to do with power and privilege, whilst the connotations of left are all loss and disease. References throughout the Bible are all symbolic and denote an inherent difference of function in the two sides of a human being, stemming through the microcosm and macrocosm relationship, from laws operating on the highest spiritual level. There is an inherent division in the God-head: that of free uncommitted power, and power tied or limited in the act of creation, so that the free, the Will of the Father, belongs to the right, and the Son, what has been born, and the Mother, the substance through which birth is possible, both belong to the left.

The right-left symbolism goes through Christian art: in a broad sense it is good and evil. 'Right' and 'left' are of course used in the heraldic sense, not as seen by the spectator. The sun and moon (q.v.), for instance, are respectively at the right and left of Christ on the cross, and Christ sits at the right hand of God the Father. In representations of the Last Judgement, those who have elected to go the way of Christ are taken up to his right, whilst the condemned are consigned to hell on his left. The Book of Life, the world and its destiny, is held on the left knee, whilst the blessing is given by the right hand of power.

Markedly too, the head of Christ on the cross always falls to the right side, symbolising the surrender of self-will to the Will of the Father: equally it is Christ's left leg, the fallen left side of man, that is fixed and sometimes bent under the firm right leg, the Will, on the cross. In the story of the Garden of Eden, Eve is properly placed on Adam's left, for she represents the loss of power in the will to the feelings and the material world. Again in the church itself, the minister, as representative of God, is in the pulpit on the north side, and the lectern containing the Word (the Book again) is on the south. In effigies of the crusaders, the left leg is for a certain Period, crossed under the right, a mnemonic that the ego has been sacrificed to the Higher Will.

ROCOCO

Probably adapted from French *rocaille*, 'rock work', since rock work features along with scroll and shell ornamentation as part of the florid and over-profuse style now known as rococo. This followed on from, and is characteristic of, the fashion of the period of Louis XV. The name, along with Baroque, tended to be used in a denigratory manner, but is now more accepted as a period with its own special value. Subject matter and treatment, in poetry and architecture, were pastoral and delicate. The period is between 1700 and 1750, and Watteau and Boucher are the names most associated with it.

ROMAN CEMENT

The early 19th century was the grand period of restoration of the English cathedrals. The so-called 'Roman' cement was often used indiscriminately, and was a composition of small fragments of stone, marble, brick and so on, mixed up with lime.

ROMANESQUE

This term denotes architecture, based on Roman art, which extended from A.D. 475 (the end of the Roman Empire) to the end of the 13th century, when the Gothic style took over.

During the 10th to the 12th centuries, there was a change from the inert solidity of the Roman tradition to problems of structural equilibrium, a delicate play of thrust and counter-thrust found in the Gothic cathedrals of the 13th century.

Middle English *rod*, 'cross'; Saxon *roda*, 'cross'. The rood is the large crucifix on the screen above the entrance to the chancel showing Christ in mortal agony; it was the focal point of the pre-Reformation church.

Early in the Middle Ages, two pulpits (ambos), one on either side of the choir, were used for readings at the Eucharist, but later this was superseded by the choir screen (the 'pulpitum' of the cathedral) over which was a loft, used in the same way, for readings and the chanting of the Gospel. The loft supported a large wooden rood showing Christ crucified, usually with the Virgin Mary and St. John on either side. This was the pattern in the parish churches until the time of the Reformation when religious intolerance, and then the Civil War, caused most of the roods and screens to be destroyed.

Such screens and lofts in cathedrals and parish churches differed in that those in cathedrals were of stone and had two staircases enabling the gospeller and the reader to move freely to and from their own side of the choir. Those in parish churches were of wood and had only one staircase, usually built in a pillar at one side: naturally it was these that were most vulnerable and suffered the most.

Symbolically the rood is the Tree of Death, the tree of suffering: but a conscious sacrificial death is the condition and cause of a new life, and the second crucifix, upon the altar, representing that Tree of Life, is properly one that shows Christ crowned as King with radiating aureole. At the present time, a plain cross is usually found on the altar, but this misses an essential symbolism. The whole idea of the rood is connected with the 'rod' of Self-authority, for through sacrifice, the root or rude power in man can ultimately be raised on the cross as regenerated spirit. (See the next entry, 'chancel' 'cross', 'Jesse tree'.)

ROOD-LOFT

A raised gallery over a rood-screen. The rood-screen is also called a rood-loft when it supports the large 'rood' or cross. The actual beam, which is sometimes above the loft supporting the cross, is in the medieval church a simple horizontal bar. The loft was reached by stairs in the wall of the chancel or in a pillar, and prior to the Reformation was also used by musicians playing on festive occasions. These stairs can be

Beam

Rood

Rood loft

Rood screen

found in many parish churches, but the screens and lofts themselves were mutilated at the Reformation.

A rood-loft is also called a *jubé*, French, from Latin *jubere*, 'to command', the first word of the Latin prayer 'Jube domine benedicere', said before the reading of the Gospel from the rood-loft.

ROOD-SCREEN

'Screen' is from Middle English *scren*, 'screen'. The idea in the screen is that of protection and concealment. The rood-screen separates the nave from the chancel, the nave being the place of the people, and the chancel containing the sanctuary, the place of the priesthood, of the inner mysteries. (See 'rood' and 'chancel'.)

ROSE

Latin *rosa*, Greek *rhodon*, 'rose'. On one level, the rose is the Mystic Rose, that flower of the spirit attainable by man through sacrifice. This is the Christ level of being. The idea of sacrifice is seen in the thorn that readily draws blood, in guarding the prize, and in the five petals that represent the five senses that have to be overcome. The idea of development which the rose symbolises is seen in the way it transmutes food from the earth to become the beautifully scented flower: in the same way basic energies in man may become transmuted to effect a spiritual rebirth.

On another level the rose is symbolic of the developing

world, the Rosa Mundi (Rose of the World), and is then connected with *rota*, 'the wheel of being'. Such a rose is connected with the Virgin Mary, the material sea, the womb in which all develops and out of which the Christ is ultimately born.

Whichever aspect, the rose denotes development, the purpose of life itself. It is used thus, and in all these senses, in the Rosicrucian rose where it is placed at the very point of transfixion on the cross. Equally, it is seen in the East as the lotus flower (the womb) within which the Buddha is shown seated and enlightened.

ROSE WINDOW

A round window with tracery radiating out from a centre, found in many cathedrals in the west façade, especially in Europe. It often has twelve divisions corresponding to the twelve astrological types. Its symbolism is described under the headings 'east end', 'rose', and 'disciples'. At the west end is the nave – the ship that saves the souls of men on the sea of life: the rose is the symbol of development in that sea which has to take place before the mysteries of the sanctuary at the east end may be realised. The lancet window is male and the rose female – an extension of the line and circle which together give the number ten, the number of ordinal perfection, signifying in man the union of spirit and matter.

ROUND TOWERS

These towers, found in Irish monastic settlements, were built in the 8th and 9th and into the 10th centuries. They were essentially places of refuge, look-out towers, belfries and hiding places for valuables at the time of the Norse invasions. They are found in areas that suffered from such invasions. Composed of five or six storeys, the lowest one is inaccessible except by ladder, which points to their function as a place of refuge. Many stand in as perfect a condition as when they were built, a testimony to the immaculate masonry of the day.

RUBRIC

Latin *rubrica*, 'red earth' or 'title of law written in red'. *Ruber*, 'red'. Hence also law. The rubric can mean either a heading, or a chapter in an illuminated manuscript, or a specific directive (usually emphasised by red writing) concerning a liturgy in the prayer book.

Old English *rūn*, 'mystery, secret', from Old High German *rūnēn*, 'to whisper'. An ancient system of writing, angular in style, belonging to the Anglo-Saxons, Scandinavian and ancient Germanic peoples. Derived from the Greek alphabet, it had added symbols and was adapted for incising into stone. The writing on the crosses and stones are of a memorial nature, as with ogham stones, containing the names of deceased and dedicator. Like ogham, the alphabet is divided into three groups, the number of letters varying with the period and known as Frey's family, Hagel's family and Tyr's family – from F, H, and T the first letters of each group. The first six letters, F U Th O R C, constitute the alternate name 'futhorc' by which the runic alphabet is known.

The writing has an early association with Christianity, being found on stone crosses and slabs – the Bewcastle and Rothwell crosses are particularly notable. Often Latin capitals are on the slabs, showing the merging of the two elements. The original meaning of the word clearly shows the use of runes in a magical context – for invocations and divination, for the evoking of beneficent and malevolent forces.

S

SACRAMENT

Latin *sacramentum*, 'oath, solemn obligation', *sacrare*, 'to set apart as sacred, dedicate', *sacer*, 'sacred'. Originally used as a Roman military oath not to desert post or standard, it was later used ecclesiastically as a translation of the Greek word *mystērion*, 'mystery', and meaning 'that which is kept sacred', a 'secret'. The origin of the Latin *sacer* is said to be doubtful, but see later in this entry.

Generally, 'sacrament' signifies one of the rites recognised and employed by the Church. Confirmation, Matrimony, Penance, Orders and Extreme Unction, are now accepted as traditional and two others, Baptism and the Eucharist, were ordained by Christ himself. Of these the latter is the most momentous, and is simply called the Sacrament or the Blessed Sacrament. In all cases a visible outer form or agency is used to confer a spiritual grace upon man, to effect a link between

God and man through the specific use of the material form along with words of power. In Baptism for example, water is used as a purifying agent for the feeling life.

But such occasions set apart as holy are ideally ratifications of some new inner state achieved by the person involved. The Sacrament or Holy Communion really belongs to the understanding that everything in life is divine in that it is a formulation of spirit. This is the deepest secret. It is the idea implied in the word *sacred*, the *sa* part being Sanskrit for 'spirit' or 'breath', and *cra* or *car* deriving from Latin *creare*, 'to create, cause to grow', from an Aryan base *ker*, *kor*, 'to grow': it says that all exists in all – that one life form depends upon another for its existence in a vast scheme of mutual eating and sacrificing; that all is holy, being of one whole. A sacrament exists to remind people that a conscious commital to a new direction, away from the error of separateness, is necessary for grace to be granted from a higher level. (See 'sacrarium'.)

SACRARIUM

Latin *sacer*, 'sacred' – see in the above entry. The sacrarium is the part of the chancel within the altar rails, the most secret place, for Christ's grace is given here to all who are truly enacting their own sacrifice and atonement. In this place the hands open to give away 'self' and at the same time receive grace. All the spiritual force in the church is concentrated in the sacrarium. In the same way, seen in the sense of the regeneration of the lower energies, all is concentrated in the head of the human being.

The key to the form of the church is seen in this analogy, in the transformation of matter into spirit, lower into higher energies. That such a process is connected with the primary energy of sex is suggested in the word 'sacrum', from the same root as *sacer*, the so-called sacred bone, triangular in shape and lying at the base of the spine. It was used anciently in sacrificial rituals with this knowledge. Thus too there is the division in the church – the symbolic rood screen (q.v.) protecting the sacred area from the nave, from the profanisation of mixing it with a lower level. (See 'chancel' 'east end', 'west end'.)

SACRISTY AND SACRIST

Latin *sacer*, 'holy'. The room adjoining a church where sacred vessels and garments are kept. The term applies only to cathedrals. The 'sacrist' of a cathedral or monastery was also the official keeper of books and music. (See 'vestry'.)

SAGGITARY

See under 'centaur'.

SAINT

Latin *sanctus*, 'holy'. The root *sa* in Sanskrit is 'spirit' or 'breath'. Pure spirit is essentially whole and unvitiated: thus Latin *sanus*, 'sound, healthy'. A saint is one in whom the interests of self have been effaced and in whom the pure spirit operates without hindrance.

SALMON

Latin *salmo*, connected with *salire*, 'to jump': the *mon* part is connected with *mono*, 'alone'. The salmon has been used from early Christian times, because of its unique life struggle, to suggest the spirit of man moving against the stream and returning to the source whence it came.

SANCTUARY

Latin *sanctus*, 'holy': thus a holy place or shrine, but especially the most secret part of a place of worship. In the church it is that part of the church east of the nave – the place of the clergy. Its meaning is discussed under 'sacrarium' and 'presbytery'.

The word has come to denote generally a place of refuge because, under ecclesiastical law in this country, fugitives from justice in the Middle Ages could, upon reaching the holy place, take refuge and claim immunity for a certain length of time. This was called the 'right of sanctuary'. (See 'frith stool'.)

SANCTUARY KNOCKER

A heavy bronze knocker, often beautifully designed, on a door at the west end of some cathedrals – a reminder of the use of the privilege of sanctuary. (See 'frith stool' and 'sanctuary'.)

SANCTUARY LAMP

The sanctuary lamp hangs from the roof of the church, a little way in front of and central to the altar, and is always lit so long as the Sacrament (the consecrated bread and wine used at the Eucharist) is present. The permanently burning light denotes the ever present spirit of God.

SANCTUS BELL

Sanctus, 'holy'. A bell used at solemn moments of the Mass, as when the Host is raised after consecration. A small handbell is now used, and was generally used prior to the Reformation. Often however the sanctus bell is housed in a turret on the outside of the church, between nave and chancel, and is rung from the inside.

SARCOPHAGUS

A Latin word from Greek *sarkophagos*, 'flesh-eating'. From *sarx*, 'flesh' and *phagein*, 'to eat'. Originally so-named because of a type of limestone, used by the Greeks in the making of coffins, which was said to allow the flesh to disintegrate quickly. The general meaning is now of a large stone coffin, or a structure erected above a grave of similar form, containing inscriptions relevant to the deceased.

SATAN

Latin, from Greek *Satanas*, Hebrew *Sātān*, 'the adversary, the accuser'. The arch-enemy of man, synonymous with the devil, having animal attributes and represented in Christian art as luring men into the pit of hell. The satanic forces are those accumulated from the repeated errors of fallen man who has leaned his will towards the material world and to his own separate existence. Such an accumulation is a living reality, a reservoir of monstrous proportions on the subtle planes, ready to lend its powers to those who offer themselves to it. On the other hand, the separate existence, and suffering attendant upon it, are the whetting stone for his spiritual development. (See 'devil' and 'lucifer'.)

SAXON (CHURCHES)

Latin *saxo*, from west Germanic *seax*, 'knife', 'sword' – a weapon used by that tribe. The Saxons along with the Angles and Jutes migrated to Britain in the 5th and 6th centuries, and the term is loosely used in architecture to denote the period from then until the Norman invasion in the 11th century.

The churches of the Saxon period were built in the north under the influence of Irish missionaries, contrasting with the basilican-type churches of the south introduced by St. Augustine. They were modelled more on the hermit cell (the 'beehive') which gradually assumed a square shape – for instance in the oblong sanctuary and square west end tower. Monk Wiermouth (Sunderland) and St. Paul's (Jarrow) are two of the finest examples of churches which were built by St. Aidan circa 635, and modified later by Benedict Biscop and St. Wilfrid.

Up to the Danish invasions of the 9th century was also the age of inscribed and ornamental sepulchral stones. The pre-Christian Saxon erected mounds of earth and buried personal possessions with the body, but Christianity brought inscribed memorial stones, erect crosses, carved Hiberno-Saxon orna-ments and runes on hog-back stones. Latin capitals and Saxon miniscules (q.v.) intermingled.

At the Synod of Whitby (664), a compromise was evolved between the basilica and Celtic forms; for instance the square presbytery was retained, but transepts and side entrances were added and the choir was separated from the nave. In the grafting of the Romanesque onto the Saxon buildings (these latter were largely made of wood), Saxon balusters, quoins and pilaster, suggesting the design of the carpenter, com-mingled with characteristic Roman brick work. Small win-dows in the west tower were a reminder of the Irish oratories. (q.v.).

From the purely religious point of view, at the Synod of Whitby, the Roman influence with its external dogmas and disciplines spelt the death of the Celtic monastic traditions. The former, through St. Paul, had remained in the Mediterra-nean area focusing on Rome, thus coming to southern Eng-land; the other had originated with the Desert Fathers focus-ing on Alexandria and, spreading to Ireland, had come to the Saxon north of England.

SCALLOP

Old French *escalope*, derived from the word *scale* which is from Old Higher German *skāla*, 'drinking cup', and Old Nor-wegian *skal*, 'shell' or 'husk'. Shell and skull are related words: both were anciently used as drinking cups. The scal-lop shell is a badge of the pilgrims who had been to the Holy Land, since it is said that these shells were found in abundance on the shores and were used as drinking cups and eating vessels. It also specifies, for the same reason, the emblem of the pilgrims to the shrine of St. James of Compostella in Spain. Architecturally, the scallop motif is found mostly in Norman capitals.

150

SCULPTURE

The characteristic of medieval church sculpture was its anonymity: moreover building and sculpture were not separable, and because all was the work of the mason, there was a homogeneity between the architecture and the figures adorning it. In the 13th century after a period of considerable heaviness, complete mastery was achieved over the material, and sculpture became the pride of the outer and inner faces of the church. In the 14th century, though the style was more decorative, work was still within the framework of the community of masons on the site. After the Black Death (14th century), figure sculpture ceased to be carried out on the site, the function of the mason changed, and work was carried out in quarry centres, as at Bristol and York. This incurred an inevitable division between the building and the work grafted onto the building.

SEDILIA

Latin, plural of *sedila*, 'seat, stool', from the root *sed,* 'sit'. The sedilia are a set of seats, made of stone and recessed into the south wall of the chancel. They are usually three in number since they are intended for the use of priest, deacon and

subdeacon during the Mass. Sometimes however, there are only two or even one, an indication of the wealth of the church. Sedilia are often at different levels, and the canopies beautifully decorated.

SEE

Old French *se, sie*, from Latin *sedes,* 'seat'. Thus it is the geographical area over which a bishop presides or has his seat.

From the past participle of Latin *sepelire*, 'to bury'. A representation of the entombment of Christ was practised each Easter in the church, when a wooden imitation of a sepulchre was erected on the north of the chancel. These have not stood the test of time, but in some parish churches the original permanent construction of stone designed to contain the sepulchre can be found. The finest of these have the elaborate ornamentation of the Decorated Period.

SERPENT

Latin *serpent*, 'snake', from *serpere*, 'to crawl or creep', related to Greek *herpein*, 'to creep'. The serpent is symbolic of the powers of evil because it represents power that has been reduced to the level of the earth. On this level, man's will is divided – he is deluded by the duality inherent in the world of the senses and time. The subtlety of the serpent in Genesis is the trickery in that duality which leads him towards what is pleasurable and away from what is painful. In this sense he weighs up 'yes's and no's' with a subtle reason, represented by the forked tongue of the serpent.

The will is thus crucified in time and made impotent. This is symbolised by the serpent twined around the cross of limitation. (Note the connection between the senses and reason: Greek *pente* is 'five' and Latin *pensare*, 'to weigh out, think'.) The serpent is synonymous with Satan in the Christian myth and in Revelation is called 'the dragon, that old serpent called the Devil which deceiveth the world'. In iconography, St. George and St. Michael are represented in combat with it.

The serpent is fundamentally power or energy in a fallen state, and thus epitomises evil; yet it has the capacity for self-regeneration as when it sheds its old skin and acquires a new one. It is then a healing force, and appeared as Aesculapius, the Greek god of healing. It is also the raised, brazen serpent of Moses, which gave life to those who looked upon it, and it is the serpent force of Yogic teaching, Kundalini, which resurrected from the lower sex energies appears reinstated in its true seat of power, the head. In Byzantine work, Christ's body on the cross assumes a serpent-like undulation, showing that he has taken upon himself the old serpent and raised it up regenerated – the new Adam out of the old.

In front of the altar of larger churches, seven lamps hang from the roof. This tradition derives from the words of the Apocalypse, 'And there were seven lamps of fire burning before the Throne which were the Seven Spirits of God'. 'Seven' can be seen as 's-even' or spirit-even or complete, for such a division of unity is found throughout the whole of nature.

The seven-branched candlestick, the seven churches of Asia, the seven days of creation, the seven colours of the rainbow, the seven tones of the musical scale, the seven major planets, the seven years in the fairy tale, are all part of this universal seven-fold structure. Each is a differentiation of the root power of God working in its own unique way. Seen from the point of view of the evolution of man, we have the seven races and the seven sub-races, and, on a smaller scale, a reflection of this in the seven yearly periods of a man's life, each of which is marked by some physiological and psychological change.

In Church doctrine there are the seven 'virtues' and their counterpart the 'deadly sins', and on the subtle plane (the seven churches of Asia in the Apocalypse can be interpreted this way), they are the vortices of power located along the spine and known in Yogic metaphysics as 'chakras'.

Upon seven stages being absorbed into one, that is, the process completed, a new octave begins. This is the eighth point. The glyph of the number eight represents the birth of a new cycle, and thus of eternity, because each end only gives way to a new beginning. (See 'font' and 'baptism'.)

SHAFT

Old High German *scaft*, 'shaft of an arrow, pole'; Latin *scapus*, 'shaft, stem', Greek *skēptein*, 'to support with a pole'. In architecture it is the main part of a column between the capital and base; but the term 'shafts' applies particularly to smaller columns clustered round pillars. In Early English work, for example, they are separate and of different material, often Purbeck marble. Such shafts vary in style according to the period.

SHRINE

Latin *scrinium*, 'case, box for papers, books and letters'. Connected with Latin *scribere*, 'to write'. A shrine in this sense is a cover for the bible of a saint, but it came to denote any case or covering for a venerated relic, as in the Irish

Church where richly ornamented metal casings were made to protect the bible, bell and crozier.

A shrine has also come to mean that part of a church where such a relic is kept – and thus any place made sacred by holy events. The shrines of the saints in the cathedrals were places of pilgrimage, originally crypts where bones were preserved. It was only later that they were brought into the body of the church, where, due to the immense quantity of wealth deposited near them, careful guard had to be kept. The elevated watch-rooms through which the shrine could be observed can be seen in many English cathedrals.

SOFFIT or SUFFIT

Italian *soffita*, 'ceiling', meaning 'fastened under' (Latin, past participle *suffixum* of *suffigere*, 'to fasten under'.) A soffit or suffit refers to the underside of an arch, or of any part of a building where an underface is in evidence, as in the ceiling of a vault, the underside of a cornice, or the transom of a window or door.

SPANDREL

Old French *espandre* from Latin *expandere*, 'to spread out, unfold'. A spandrel is the triangular space between arches. The word is also used to denote an irregular, uncommitted surface, as between the arch and cusp of a window, or between the ribs of a vault.

SPIRE

Old English and Middle English *spir*, 'spire', from Old Norwegian *spira*, 'point' or 'ear of corn'. Thus through the image, the prolongation of a tower tapering to a point. There are obvious connections with Latin *spira*, from Greek *speira*, 'coil, twist'; also with Latin *spirare*, 'to breath', giving the word spirit. All have some connection with the essentially 'aspiring' spire which is a visible expression of the spiritual zeal that gave rise to the Gothic cathedrals.

The placing of the spire in the cathedrals and churches is over the central tower, at the place of the crossing, in a sense the crux of the church form. (See 'lantern tower' and 'transepts' for symbolism.)

154

SPLAY

Middle English *splayen*, 'to spread outwards'; splay is an abbreviated form of display. It means the sloping, bevelled jambs of a window, spreading out to make a larger opening on the inside wall of a building. (See under 'window'.)

SQUINT

Middle English *asquint*, from Old Frisian *schün*, 'oblique'. A hole cut obliquely in the wall of a medieval church, for instance in the transepts or side chapels, allowing the high altar to be seen from where it would otherwise not be visible. Squints vary in width and style in different parts of the country. They also bear the name 'hagioscope', a word which indicates their function more clearly – *hagios*, Greek, 'holy, pertaining to saints', and *skopos*, Greek, 'watcher, spy'.

STAINED GLASS

Until about the middle of the 12th century, images were painted upon walls and vaults in churches. From the cells of the hermits to the later monastic buildings, there had been little window space. But as the balance changed in favour of light, the use of coloured glass began to flourish. The first known instance is in the west front of Chartres Cathedral (middle 12th century), though presumably the technique had been known prior to this time. Scenes from the Old Testament and the lives of the saints were depicted, replacing the wall paintings. The effect of brilliant light in the colours was the result of using thick pot glass, full of bubbles, irregularities and chemical impurities.

Early windows, such as Canterbury and York, were made of small pieces of glass leaded together and were of rich ruby, blue, maroon and green. They were largely single figures of medallion form, and in the aisles so they could be studied by the people. After 1170 a technique called 'grisaille' (q.v.) was introduced; it was a grey-green type of glass with simple geometric patterns and only a little coloured glass. After 1280 new techniques were developed – a technique of silver stain was discovered, and larger pieces of glass were used with windows made of three or five lights. The imagination was gradually set free. But tracery in the windows forced the glass artist to adopt his figures to the forms presented, giving awkward shapes. By the Perpendicular Period (middle of the 14th century), the glaziers' work began to assume such an importance that it is evident that stonework tracery was designed before building to fit the needs of the glazier, especially in relation to canopied figures. This period saw an increased use of heraldry and a personalising of the people and themes presented.

The decline of the art of stained glass was due primarily to the influence of painting – the attempt to paint on glass, an influence from Flanders, caused the tracery to be seen as an obstacle in the way of the painter's conception. The 16th century was the time of the decline of glass and the rise of painting.

STALLS

Old English *steall*, 'stall, stable', Old High German *stall*, 'stable'. The meaning is a division or compartment in a stable; thus a similar division or recess in the form of a seat in a church. The stalls for the choir in a cathedral may be allotted to particular church dignitaries; the bishop especially has his own stall or 'throne', distinguished by its particularly fine carving.

The choir stalls contain some of the finest examples of medieval woodwork, and are known for their misericords, the secondary under-seats of each stall carved with mythological animals and contemporary scenes. (See 'misericord'.) The term was more generally applied to the wooden divisions erected in parish churches for the more privileged families of the congregation. (See 'pew'.)

STANCHION

Latin *stare*, 'to stand'. A vertical iron bar between the stone mullions in a window. The term is sometimes used for the mullion itself.

STAR OF DAVID

The interlacing of two triangles gives a six-pointed star often found in church iconography, a reference to the lineage of Christ through King David, described in the Old Testament. To the Hebrews it symbolised the triune God (Father, Mother and Son) reflected in His own creation.

The triangle with its base below, called the Macroprosupus, 'great countenance', is the divine triangle, light, and a symbol of fire, indicating energy raying downwards, encompassing and sustaining all below. The triangle with its base uppermost, called the Microprosupus, 'small countenance', is the triangle of man and nature, dark, and the symbol of God's power reflected in the waters of chaos. In this triangle, man aspires upwards from the insecure particularised point to embrace infinity. He can only become stabilised however, by attuning his three-fold nature (will, heart, head) to the Higher Trinity, and the interlaced triangles are not merely God reflected in his creation, but, reciprocally, man's desire to return to the light of the spirit. It is thus a symbol of such a potential state in all men.

When the glyph has a dot in the centre, it is known as Solomon's Seal – that is the healing of the divinity, the seventh point, within a man – a seal of completion.

The Star of David has of course many aspects, but it is basically to do with the union of spirit and matter, God and man, male and female, all of which are to do with the division inherent in the very act of Creation. For this reason it has always been a symbol of the Logos or the Spoken Word. The number six denotes this division (its origin is from the word *sex*, which fundamentally means division). The triangle of the Holy Trinity adopted in early Christianity has the base line uppermost, showing the support of the higher power for the lower. Here the Holy Spirit, the point of the triangle, points to the earth, egressing equally from Father and Son. (See 'Trinity'.)

STATIONS OF THE CROSS

The fourteen 'stations of the cross' belong mainly to the Roman Church. Originally varying in number, they are also called 'Via Calvaris', or 'Via crucis', and their purpose is to represent by painting, in fresco, or on canvas on the walls of the church, Christ's progression from the Judgement Hall to Calvary. They are as follows:

1 he is condemned to death
2 he is forced to carry his own cross
3 he falls under the cross
4 he meets his mother
5 Simon the Cyrenean helps him to carry his cross
6 Veronica wipes his face

7 he falls under the cross again
8 he speaks to the daughters of Jerusalem
9 he falls a third time under the cross
10 he is stripped of his garments
11 he is nailed to the cross
12 he yields up the Holy Ghost
13 he is taken down from the cross
14 he is placed in the sepulchre

Originally these points were actually in Jerusalem and used by pilgrims. Later, when the Franciscans were granted custody of the Holy Sepulchre, they erected images of these events (called 'stations') in their European churches so that pilgrimages could be done in spirit. The Dissolution of the Monasteries saw the destruction of most of the paintings of these stations that were an integral part of the pre-Reformation church.

STOUP

The stoup (Old Norwegian *staup*, Old English *stēap*, 'flagon') is a small stone vessel or basin set in the wall at the western entrance, now mainly used in a Catholic church. They were built in all pre-Reformation churches, but most have fallen into decay or have been removed entirely.

The stoup contains holy water (sometimes a fountain) which has been blessed against the force of evil. The self-crossing with holy water upon entering the church was a re-enactment of the baptism by which a member, received into the Body of the Church, was vouchsafed regeneration.

The holy water in the stoup and in the baptismal font has a two-fold consecration. First the water itself, clean but not distilled, is consecrated to banish impurities, and secondly, the essential ingredient, salt, is also consecrated. Salt is the principle of contraction, the hardening of the free energy of fire in the form of condensed earth – thus the symbol of the 'pillar of salt'. But paradoxically, the psychological contraction, the ego, has the highest possible level of awareness within it, man's real Self. The negative symbol now becomes positive, as in the expression the 'salt of the earth' and in the food we eat, for without salt, food is tasteless. Thus the priest banishes one aspect of salt to give life to the other. Such a dialectic is seen under 'cross', 'tree', 'Lucifer' and so on.

Similarly, if water is seen in this way, the waters of materiality in which man flounders are his enemy; and yet at the same time water is the most powerful of cleansers (as for that matter is salt). Again we have two faces for one symbol.

STRINGCOURSE

A thin horizontal line of moulding projecting from the wall of a building.

SUN AND MOON

The sun and moon are frequently found in representations of the Crucifixion, especially in the medieval period: the sun is to the right of the head of Christ and the moon to the left. As in all other cases where it occurs, 'right' symbolises power and good, and 'left' the forces of deprivation and evil. The symbolism occurs in the most ancient of religions.

The sun and the moon are polar opposites. The sun is an embodiment of the Intelligence of the Logos – the Son in the Trinity. 'Sun' and 'son' are by meaning deeply connected and are related etymologically to *sonare* (Latin, 'sound'), signifying the sounding out of the Word, the Logos – the intelligent ordering force in the universe. The sun is both the light of intelligence and the heat of life. The moon, on the contrary, is an embodiment of all that is to do with inertia, with the mechanical forces of nature. In most languages 'moon' means 'month' and derives from the root *me*, 'to measure'. The moon symbolises the whole material world, the death of free energy, and all opposition to the will of man.

Sun and moon are aspects of each other – the power and intelligence of the sun works in and through the moon process, the counting process of the world. When at the term of the evolutionary process the physical world is re-spiritualised, the sun and moon will be seen to have been aspects of each other and such a duality will be no more. Thus the statement in Revelation:

> And the city had no need of the sun, neither of the moon,
> to shine on it: for the Glory of God did lighten it, and the
> Lamb is the light thereof –

and the reason why they are found at either side of the head
of Christ, for since he is the sacrificial Lamb and the agent of
the re-spiritualising process, the city will be illumined by his
light.

In extension of this, the moon in Christian art is significantly a crescent moon, the beginning of that new birth, and the
rest of the sphere is only partially, that is potentially, illumined. Equally significantly, on a purely scientific level, the
sun and moon, as seen by man on earth, are of identical
dimension, a fact that corroborates what has been said about
their polar opposition.

SUPPORTER IN HERALDRY

The human or animal figures at either side of a shield ap-
parently supporting it. Such figures encouraged the creation
of an array of mythical beasts distinct from those on the
shields. They are not in evidence before the last quarter of the
14th century.

SUPPRESSION OF THE MONASTERIES

The ruined state of the abbeys and the monasteries in
Britain is almost wholly due to the event known as the Suppression of the Monasteries. The monasteries in the course of
400 years had lost their original spiritual zeal: their life had
reached its term because of wealth and general laxity in monastic rule. The original plan of Wolsey in 1528 to suppress
certain smaller houses, in order to endow the 'Cardinal Col-
lege' at Oxford, was symptomatic of the inevitable break-
down. This and other closures had the sanction of the Pope,
though the relationship between Pope and English monarchy
was deteriorating. In 1538, however, Parliament, on the suggestion of Thomas Cromwell, adviser to Henry VIII, ordered
a 'visitation' – a report on the monasteries. Eighty-eight were
visited and the result came to be known as the Black Book.
Parliament, on the strength of this report, ordered the suppression of all monasteries with an income of less than £200,
and, of course, the confiscation of their property. 376 houses in
the country were suppressed.

Two risings took place in opposition to this action: one in
Lincolnshire and one in Yorkshire. The Yorkshire one
assumed considerable proportions and was called the 'Pilgrim-

age of Grace'. It was finally put down and the abbots of Fountains, Rievaulx and Jervaulx were hanged and their monasteries given over to the king. During 1538-9, 150 other monasteries were taken over by the king in devious ways and by 1540 all extant monasteries had been suppressed and their wealth used on public welfare, as for example in the founding of grammar schools or colleges, or given to the courtiers who were favourites of the king. Those that did not succumb wholly in this way re-emerged to take their place among the already existing cathedrals.

SURPLICE

Medieval Latin *superpelliceum* (*super*, 'over' and *pelliceum*, 'tunic of skins' – *pelis*, 'skin'). The surplice is now simply a long loose robe worn by a priest not celebrating Eucharist, and also by the choir.

SWASTIKA

Sanskrit *svastis*, 'welfare', from *su*, 'well', and *asti*, 'being', which has the same source as the Greek and Latin verbs for 'to be'. The well-being implied in the symbol is that of the being of the universe or uni-verse (one turn), the wheel of life, within which lie a complexity of systems turning within each other.

Essentially a cross, the tails of the swastika depict the pattern of fire in rotation, the image of the turning Catherine-wheel. Though a universal symbol of great antiquity, it was also a Christian symbol by virtue of the fire of the sun, representing the spiritual fire of Christ. It moves in a clockwise direction, the apparent direction of the sun, but when reversed, the direction becomes 'widdershins', that is contrary to the apparent motion of the sun and thus a force of evil – thus it was the emblem, for instance, of Nazi Germany. In Europe, the swastika was anciently known as Thor's hammer, an agent for shaping the soul through the hard blows given by the whirling tails.

It is sometimes called a *fylfot* – which is generally supposed to mean 'fill the foot'. Such a motif was used as decoration in windows or in embroidery. (See 'fylfot'.)

SWAN

Old English and Saxon both have the same, *swan*. The root of the word is Latin *sonare*, 'to sound', coming from a Sanskrit root meaning 'sound' – thus the connection of the name with the myth that the swan sings (swan-song) before it dies.

But the swan makes no such death song. The sound that the myth is indicating is the original sound, French *son*, or Son of the Trinity: it is the Logos or Spoken Word, of which the sound of the senses is but the merest reflection. Thus it is essentially pure, and it is this purity that dies with the birth of the world, giving way to an earthly song described in the myth as a death-song. This is of course another version of the fall into the physical plane of existence. Also since the Word follows upon the Will of the Father, the glyph of the swan is the number 2 where the Will is the number 1. The number 3 is an egg or circle (zero) broken into two connected halves giving three points, the inter-related forces of the Trinity (q.v.).

The swan, as a bird, denotes intelligence, and its whiteness, pure intelligence; because it glides with dignity upon the surface of the water, it is also the kingly Intelligence of the Logos. When it appears in myth or heraldry, especially in certain stories about the locating of sites of monasteries by saints, the activity of the Intelligence of the Logos is always indicated.

T

TABERNACLE

Latin *tabernaculum*, 'tent', from *taberna*, 'hut, booth, dwelling'. (Note English, 'tavern'.) The basic meaning is of a portable tent used as a temple by the Israelites during their wanderings in the wilderness.

Hence the word came to mean something in which a precious or holy thing was deposited, especially, in the western Church, the ornamental receptacle for the pyx in which the consecrated Host (wafer) for use in the Eucharist is preserved. This at first hung over the altar but was later the altar itself. 'Tabernacle' is also used for the niche behind the altar, where the Host is alternatively kept. A light hangs over the altar so long as the Host is so preserved. 'Tabernacle' has also been extended to denote the niches in inner or outer walls of a church containing statues or tombs of saints. Such recesses have ornamental canopies or arches of the period, ranging from the simple shallow and square ones of the Norman period to the deeply inset, highly ornamented ones of

'Decorated' period

the Perpendicular period. The intricate carving is often called 'tabernacle-work'.

TAPESTRY

French *tapis*, 'carpet, tapestry', Latin *tapete*, 'carpet'. Tapestry is loom work and is to be distinguished from the smaller proportions of embroidery, which derives from *broder*, or *border*, 'to work the edge of'.

Tapestry was much used in the decoration of churches – for walls, and especially for the decoration of altars – from an early time. The town of Arras in Artois, France, was the first centre of manufacturing, giving the name of a type of tapestry called 'arras', woven in patterns rather like wall-paper. In the 15th century, manufacturers made religious and mythological pictures; the taste for tapestry flourished and 'hangings' were an important acquisition in the houses of the nobility. In 1607 the factory was established in Paris which later became known as the Gobelins, giving rise to the highest achievements in tapestry work.

Tapestry, like all weaving and spinning, is essentially a female activity, since it is associated with the weaving of the web of the material world, of the spell of illusion, the Hindu *maya* or cosmic spider. The Great Mother (see 'Virgin Mary') spins the world out of her own being. Thus tapestry work is associated with the principle of purity and maternity, and belongs traditionally to the Virgin Mary.

TAU CROSS or ST. ANTHONY'S CROSS

See 'cross' for the symbolism of the cross. The Tau cross, originally the Egyptian cross of life, became associated with the 4th century desert hermit St. Anthony, who was of Egyptian origin, and could be said to be the founder of the monastic system.

TEMPLE

Certain churches have the name 'temple', some through Protestant connections and some through association with the Knights Templars.

'Temple' is from Latin *templum*, 'a place or space in the sky ringed out for observation by priests or augurs in ancient Rome'. Augury was the art of divining through a study of the flight of birds in that marked out place. The Latin word is from Greek *temeos*, 'a sacred place' from *temnein*, 'to cut'. Thus the general meaning later of any consecrated place set apart for worship.

There is also the connection with Latin *tempus*, 'time', said to be of doubtful etymology. The connection between the two is in the space ringed and cut off. As in augury, where the magical proscribed area contains eternal truths to be interpreted on the time level, so time itself is cut off from the eternal level, marking itself by the endless repetitive cycles of nature. This is the ring of time which holds men enthralled. Yet eternity lives within time, and seen positively, the aim of the temple is to contain spiritual energies within the ring so that eternity can be rediscovered and experienced within the temporal.

In this sense, stone circles are temples, for within the confined circle the mysteries of the cosmos were reflected and revealed: sacred dances, too, now reflected in children's games, had this function. Man is said to be his own temple in that all his experiences in time, properly used, can lead to a new understanding and a break-back into eternity.

The connection with the Knights Templars is through the Temple of Solomon at Jerusalem, circa 1000 B.C. This was destroyed and built over several times, but the knights who devoted themselves to the protection of pilgrims used the site for their headquarters – thus acquiring their name.

TESTER

French *tête*, Latin *testa*, 'shell, skull'. A flat canopy over a pulpit or tomb or, domestically, over a bed.

TIE-BEAM

A simple beam crossing from one side of the roof to the other, tying them together by supporting the king-posts and other timber work. It was used mostly in the Norman period but continued in medieval times when the beam was often slightly curved upwards towards the centre.

TOMB

Latin *tumba*, 'a grave for burying the dead'; the word is related to *tumulus*, 'heap of earth, mound', used as a burial place: both denote confinement to earth.

The physical body is also such a tomb, for the spirit falls into it at birth, where it is held captive. This is the idea be-

Tomb

Altar

hind French *tomber*, 'to fall', as well as the idea of the body
falling into the earth at death. The tomb as commonly understood is a stone block in the form of an altar – altar because
it is here that earthly values are transformed into spiritual
ones. The imagery in the tomb, then, is that though the body
falls into the earth, is entombed at death, it does so only for
the spirit to be resurrected into eternal life. In the Eastern
Church there is a clear use of this symbolism for the altar is
seen as both the tomb of Christ and the throne of God.

Early in Christianity in Britain, saints were interred in
the crypts of cathedrals, but later, relics were brought to
ground level to become the elaborate tombs or shrines which
were the objects of veneration for pilgrims.

TOWER

Old French *tour*, Latin *turris*, 'a high tower for defence
purposes'. In English cathedrals the most imposing feature is
the central tower above the crossing. It raises itself in the form
of a spire. The tower is also known as the 'lantern tower' since
it lets light in onto the crossing. (See 'crossing' and 'transept'.)

Due to the structural problems with the position of the
central tower, it often fell down, which accounts for the many
awkward modifications and divergencies of style in later rebuilding.

TRACERY

Middle English *trācen*, through Old French, from Low
Latin *tractiare* and *trabere*, 'to draw'. Thus in the tracery –
that is the decorative stonework in the upper part of a window
– the impression is of a regular pattern drawn upon the win-

a a b c c

d d e f

dow. The use of tracery refers specifically to the windows of Gothic churches, the several names corresponding to some extent to the recognised periods, though overlapping makes exact dating impossible.

(a) *Plate tracery*: in the first half of the 13th century, when two lancet windows were made in one arch, the space remaining above was filled by a circle or quatrefoil.

(b) *Bar tracery*: about the middle of the 13th century increased piercing of stone caused a feeling that bars were creating a pattern. Thus the naming 'bar tracery' and the alternative name 'geometric'.

(c) *Flowing tracery*: about the beginning of the 14th century sinuous lines developed, with some irregularity of pattern. Heads of lights took the ogee form.

(d) *Perpendicular tracery*: soon after the middle of the 14th century, vertical bars were apparent throughout the window. The amount of the stone surface was reduced until at the end of the 14th century all curved lines had disappeared. All patterns were within vertical lines – a common feature due to the size of the window in the 'transom' or cross-bar. This remained until the end of the 15th century.

(e) *Reticulated tracery*: is the name given to the device of a repetitive pattern, and this overlaps geometric and flowing tracery.

(f) *Flamboyant tracery*: French *flambeau*, 'torch', denotes the flame-like style current in France during the Perpendicular Period in England. Though not indigenous to Britain, there was later imitation.

TRANSEPT

Latin *trans*, 'across' and *septum*, 'a hedge or enclosure'. The transept is the extension, before the choir stalls, cutting across the church at right-angles and giving the cross form of the church. Though such a form can be traced through modifications of the Roman basilica, it arose, as all forms arise, from an intuitive correspondence with its essential meaning – in this case with the core of Christianity, the cross.

The cross has always signified the transfixing of spirit in matter, of eternity in time, and, as Christ's life shows, of divinity in humanity. The sacrifice of the human part to the divine is every man's inner work in this life, and the crucial (cross) moment is the change of heart which enables this to happen.

The human body can be equated roughly with the cross and the form of the church. Symbolically, the place of the crossing is the place of the heart, above which is the 'lantern' or central tower letting in the light of understanding. Beyond this lie the mysteries of the sanctuary where, for those in whom a change has taken place, ultimate enlightenment is received in 'the place of the skull' – the literal translation of Golgotha.

TRANSITION

The term applied to the transition from the Norman to the Gothic styles, sometimes called 'the battle of the styles', between circa 1150 and 1200. It is seen as a movement towards refinement and delicacy, especially in the shaping of windows and arches, and in more slender columns, though in this period old and new often appear together. The pointed arch is said to have come from the Mohammedans in the Middle East, having been introduced via Sicily into France. It is found in use by the Cistercians, the first to adopt it, in 1150.

The change to the pointed arch was also linked with the changing architectural problems, especially of vaulting: it also reflected the spirit of religious aspiration of that time.

TRANSOM

Latin *transtrum*, 'a beam that runs from side to side in a ship'. The term now denotes the cross-beam of stone or wood across a doorway or window; it is used frequently to denote a bar or bars that cut across the middle of a window, and as such it is characteristic of the Perpendicular period.

TREE OF JESSE

(See 'Jesse Tree'.) For general symbolism of the tree, see 'Adam and Eve', 'Garden of Eden', 'cross', 'rood', 'Crucifixion'.

TREFOIL

Latin *tre*, 'three', and *foil*, Middle English 'leaf' from Latin *folium*, 'leaf'. A design, in arches and in window tracery, of three leaves. Already used in Saxon churches, the possibility is that it was of Saracen origin, as with the pointed arch and interlacing Norman arches. It became a symbol, in Christian art, of the Holy Trinity. Windows with four and five leaves respectively are known as quatrefoil and cinquefoil.

TRIFORIUM

Latin *tri*, 'three' and *foris*, 'door', or 'opening'. The term denotes the gallery of openings, found only in larger churches, immediately above the main arcades in the walls of the nave and transepts. Because it occupies a position where the roof slopes over the aisles, the gallery has no light and is often called the 'blind storey'.

The *tri* originally referred to the arcades of some Norman churches in this position, where there were three openings: later the term was applied to any gallery in this position. (See 'bay'.)

TRINITY

Latin *trinus*, 'three-fold'. It was not until the 2nd century that the word came to be used. The Christian Trinity is, as with all other trinities, a division of Absolute power: its three aspects, functionally different, yet mutually dependent, make one whole. Thus the expression 'three-in-one' – God the Father, pure generative energy; God the Son, the Word or

Logos, the idea-world ordering and conditioning that power; and God the Holy Ghost, the force reconciling the first two and giving that flow which is life itself, and, on man's level, is the grace between God and himself. (Ghost is from Old High German *gest*, 'life, spirit'.) The glyph that incorporates these elements and which is found frequently in Church iconography is given here. Deus, God at the centre, has three aspects – Pater, Filius, Spiritus – clearly shown belonging to the centre but not to each other.

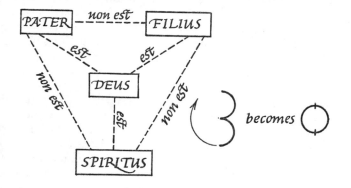

The three-in-one is also seen in the three-branched candlestick, and in the glyph of the number 3 itself, for if the semicircles are folded towards each other, the hitherto three separate points make a complete circle. (See 'swan'.)

Generally in Christian art, God the Father was only represented by a hand, his creative power, or by an eye, his all-seeing power, emerging out of clouds. Only after the 12th century was God the Father shown as a head and later as a whole body. When this occurs, he bears the orb, denoting power over the world. God the Son, more easily represented through the incarnations as Jesus Christ, is seen early in art, as a lamb, fish or vine, but mostly simply as the cross, since the cross of sacrifice denoted the uncommitted power of God transfixed by the Word. It was only in the 5th century that the crucified Christ and his suffering on the cross was represented; moreover, until the 11th century Christ was always portrayed clothed.

The Holy Spirit was always represented by a dove – the fiery dove of Pentecost, sign of reconciliation between God and man. As the embodiment of innocence and love, it rays forth its power at the baptism of Christ, at the Annunciation,

and at the creation of the world, whilst in the church building it is found over the baptismal font and over the altar.
When the Holy Spirit was represented anthropomorphically,
a scroll was held in the hand, denoting the Book of Life, the
destiny of man, though such representation was forbidden as
sacrilegious by a papal edict early in the 17th century. The
Holy Spirit was also represented, by biblical reference, as
cloven tongues of fire.

Threefold

The three aspects of the Trinity are found throughout
nature. In the archetypal tree (tri), for instance, there is an
interflow between the three parts – root, trunk and leaves.
Energy drawn in through the root rises up the trunk in the
form of the sap, and nourishes the flower and leaves. Correspondingly, man consists of will, feeling and thinking and
ideally is a perfect reflection of the Holy Trinity, but he has
been made imperfect by the fall and abuses his powers.
The root power is biased towards sexuality, the heart is
directed towards self-love, head has become a mere instrument of rational thought and a recorder of data, and all three
are closely tied to egotism, man's need to do all for his own
gain. The true functioning of the root power results in immediate action of tremendous power, of the heart a compassion for all men and for all creation, and of the head a true
logic which sees the relationship of all parts in the whole and
thus the folly of separation. Since a man's will, heart, and
head have a complex inter-working, there is much confusion
in him and harmony only comes from a re-appraisal and re-
training which leads to singleness of intent – an intent to be
an instrument of higher powers and a true reflection of the
Three in One. ('Thy Will be done in Earth as it is in Heaven'.)
The blessing (q.v.) made by the thumb and two fingers is a
symbol of the Trinity, and represents such a connection between God and man.

TRIPTYCH

Greek *triptykhos*, literally 'three-folds', *tri*, 'three' and
ptykhē, 'layer, fold'. A carving or painting done on three
panels, especially meant to serve as a reredos and thus found
immediately behind the altar. It is sometimes called an 'altarpiece'. Its three-foldness symbolises the Holy Trinity.

TRIQUETRA

Latin feminine of *triquetrus* (*tri*, 'three' and *quetrus*, 'sharp,
pointed'). It is an ornament found on very early northern

monuments, as in Celtic crosses, formed of three interlacing almond shapes and symbolising the Trinity.

TRUMPET

Middle English *trumpe*, French *trompe*, derived from Latin *triumphus*, 'triumph' and Greek *thriambos*, 'procession to Bacchus'.

In Church iconography, angels are often seen blowing trumpets (seemingly inapposite instruments compared to the gentler harp with which they also associated). This is because the sound of the trumpet symbolises the ruthlessness of the Day of Judgement and the final triumph of good over evil. It is 'the last trump'; and as in the card game where the trump card is left face upwards for all to see, all will be revealed and each being consigned to his own place according to his works. Thus the words in Matthew, 'and he shall send his angels with a trumpet and a great voice, and they shall gather his elect . . .'

The seven trumpet calls in the Apocalypse (q.v.) announce the stages of liberation from the lower forces in the unveiling process, and indicate the importance of sound in the higher worlds.

TUDOR PERIOD

The period following on the Perpendicular and roughly equated with the first half of the 16th century – 1485 to 1558. The style was a continuation of the Perpendicular, plus the revived classical forms which had spread through France in the spirit of the Renaissance. The craftsmen of the Gothic tradition worked under the guidance of classically trained and orientated artists. Much of this style is to be found in domestic architecture but ecclesiastical tombs and monuments have clear indications of the grafting process.

TYMPANUM

Latin from Greek *tympanon*, 'kettle-drum', from *typtein*, 'to strike'. In Greek architecture, a tympanum is the area of the triangular recessed face of a pediment at the end of a building: in medieval cathedrals it is the space between the lintel and the arch over doorways. In whichever period, there is the image of the tension of the skin of the drum, an image that has passed also into the naming of the membrane of the ear. In Greece, the tension was between the opposing forces of energy and reason, of earth (base of triangle) and sun forces

Greece

Ely, circa
1140

pulling upwards (point of triangle): in temples the space was
covered with richly decorated sculpture and was recognised as
the crowning achievement of the building. In the medieval
cathedral, the tension was between the inertia of the earth and
the aspiring spirit, a characteristic of the cathedral as a whole
(see 'cathedral'). It is also a characteristic of any true religious
process, where the aim of the free spirit is to become reconciled to the physical cage by which it is constrained. On the
Continent, the main west door of cathedrals has a tympanum,
invariably with the theme of the Last Judgement, the sum-
ming up of the work done, and here, as in Greece, the sculpture was the pride of the cathedral. Though tympani are
found in small churches, with one or two exceptions they are
not a feature of English cathedrals. (See 'pediment'.)

U

UNCIAL

Latin *uncialis*, 'to do with an ounce or an inch'. St. Jerome
referred to very large letters of ancient biblical scripts by the
words 'litterae unciales': the term refers now to such capitals,
though not necessarily an inch high, used by the Greeks for
inscriptions and sacred writings of importance. They are different in character from normal capitals and are found in
biblical texts of the 4th to the 9th centuries. It was only in

the 9th century that a smaller 'cursive' script (cursive means 'running together') was used in the writing of texts.

UNCTION

Latin *unctio*, 'anointing with oil'. Consecrated olive oil used in certain rites for the healing of maladies, physical or spiritual; and in the Roman and Orthodox Churches, 'extreme unction' is the applying of oil to the physical body of the dying – eyes, ears, nose, mouth, hands, feet and thighs (seven in all, the first five being the organs of the senses).

The power of oil is inherent in the term 'Christ'. Its function is a healing one, since on the material plane it is the counterpart of love. Everywhere it eliminates friction and its application is an act of relationship, love and reconciliation between God and man – it is a consecration or making holy, seen even today in the coronation ceremony where the monarch is anointed with oil. This function applies equally in other church rituals and occurs universally in mythology.

UNDERCROFT

Croft is from Old High German *chruft*, which is from Latin *crupta*, *crypta*, whence 'crypt'. Thus the same meaning as crypt – a vaulted room under a church.

UNICORN

Latin *unu*s, 'one' and *cornus*, 'animal horn'. The one-horned mythical beast represented in medieval Christian art. It is traditionally said to lay itself down at the feet of a virgin, and in art the unicorn and the virgin are frequently seen together. This is because it is a symbol, through the horn that screws itself into a single point, of the pure undivided will from which the duality of the world has been expunged. As Christ was born of a virgin (the Virgin Mary, literally the pure sea, the material sea), so the Christ-state in all men is attained through the regeneration of the body, that is a reversal of all values normally given to the world of the senses. Only after such a birth has taken root can the will become single in being given over to the Will of God.

In heraldry, the lion and the unicorn are the well known supporters of the English shield, but the unicorn was only introduced in 1603. At this date, James VI of Scotland caused one of the two unicorns which were the supporters of the Scottish shield, to supplant the Red Dragon of Wales.

Latin *urna*, 'pitcher'. It is a vessel which contained the ashes of the dead in Roman times. The urn was re-introduced in art at the Renaissance and is often found in church monuments.

USE

Latin *usus*, 'custom, usage'. A 'use' is ecclesiastically a particular liturgy established in early Christianity in this country. Upon Augustine arriving in England and finding the country already Christianised, the conflict arose as to whether to adopt the prevailing liturgy or to impose his own Roman use. Pope Gregory's response indicated compromise in the words – 'instil this [the compromise] into the minds of the Angles for their use'.

Thus the term 'Augustine's new use' is basically the British liturgy. Later bishops attempted to re-affirm the Roman liturgy, each according to his preference. Thus, the Use of York, Exeter, Lincoln, etc. The Sarum Use, formulated in 1085 at Salisbury, replaced many of the original ones, and in 1549 the Book of Common Prayer affirmed only one 'use' in the whole realm.

V

VAULT

Low Latin *vulta* or *voluta*, from past participle of Latin *volvere*, 'to roll'. Thus the image of an arch or a series of arches as in a vaulted ceiling; and also the image of the vault as a leap which has the same arched form. The other vault with an arched roof found in churches is the underground chamber containing coffins.

VESTRY

Latin *vestiarium*, 'cupboard for clothes, chest', from *vestis*, 'garment, clothing', from Greek and Sanskrit roots. A room attached to a church where the vestments of the clergy and liturgical vestments are put on: it is also used for conducting Church business. In a cathedral it is called a sacristy (q.v.).

VICAR

Latin *vicarius*, 'a deputy, substitute'. This term was brought about at the Dissolution of the Monasteries when many of the tithes, customarily the right of the rector, were sold off. The vicar of a parish is technically one who has been appointed in place of a rector and who has no right to the payment of these tithes. Presently, the term vicar is loosely used to mean the incumbent of a parish, or any man in holy orders.

VINE

Vinum, 'vine', from a root *vi*, 'to bend, twine', as in *viere*, 'to bend or twist'. The symbol of the vine and the vine leaf is found frequently in Christian art, because of Christ's words 'I am the true vine . . .'.

The vine, in the ramification of its branches, is the archetype of the Tree of Life. The blood system and nervous system of the human body, and the image of the ancestral tree, are all similar ramifications. When wine is drunk to represent the sacrificed blood of Christ at the Eucharist, we see the isolated man as a re-affirmed branch of the whole spiritual tree. We also see a suggestion of the real significance of wine.

Wine has the capacity to disorientate totally the mechanism of the physical body, a fact normally regarded in a negative light. In doing so, however, it also relaxes the restrictions of the empirical ego and reaches a more real part of a human being. The function of wine lies in this fact, that it cuts through a man's egotism and, in this sense, wine is a symbol of the pure spirit which, once it is allowed to operate, penetrates the erroneous areas of his psyche and reclaims him as part of the whole vine. Then he may be said to be drunk with spirit. Nor is it surprising on this account that wine is associated with the 'blood' of the Eucharist, for, on a subtle level, the blood mediates between spirit and body in a man. (See 'blessing'.)

VOLUTE

Latin *voluta*, past participle of *volvere*, 'to roll'. Thus the spiral scroll motif which figures principally in Ionic and also Corinthian capitals. It is retained in Norman capitals but was later supplanted by Early English foliage.

As the mother of Christ, the Virgin Mary figures prominently in Church iconography; but she is essentially the Great Mother of all mythologies. *Mary* is from Latin *mare*, 'sea', and signifies the sea or matrix from which all matter sprang.

The given etymology of the word 'virgin' is not satisfactory: Latin *virago*, 'a man-like woman', gives a clue to the real meaning of the word. Male *vir* 'man' and *gin*, connected with birth, as in genesis through Greek *gunē*, 'woman', indicates on a deep level, a state of oneness in which male and female aspects of God are still undivided. In this state, the Virgin Mary is Bride of God, Sophia, or unstained Wisdom: but upon the male spirit moving upon the face of the water and the Word being made flesh, virginity in its true sense is lost, the world was made. Separated from her male consort, the female unformed sea was reduced to the material plane.

On the material plane, the division is reflected in the human male-female opposition, with male retaining a shadow of female and female a shadow of male, physiologically and psychologically. In the ordinary meaning of the word, a virgin, either male or female, is one who has not surrendered to the external stimulus of the other half. The Virgin Mary is the perfected being through whose womb the descent of God as man could take place; she is a virgin in that her body was ready to be a servant to her will, substance a servant to spirit, and therefore whole.

In the sense that the woman, the material body, the mother of life, was originally the unformed substance or field-forces awaiting impregnation, she is as was said, 'without stain'. She is potentially Immaculate Wisdom, and this is symbolised by the pure light blue of the clothing of the Virgin. In the sense that all life is possible only through her, Mary, and all mothers, aim to give birth to a Christ child, for each physical body contains a spirit whose end is to realise Christhood through terrestrial experience. This is why, next to Christ, the Virgin Mary is the most frequently depicted figure and regarded with the greatest reverence.

VOUSSOIR

French word akin to *voute*, 'vault', and through this connection, meaning any of the wedge-shaped stones forming an arch, as above a door. The stone above the centre of the arch is called the 'key-stone'.

W

WALL PAINTING

From Norman times, much colour was used in the decorating of church walls. Norman doorways, arches and piers were all coloured in patterns similar to the pattern of the mouldings. What traces remain suggest that walls may have been covered by figures and geometric designs giving a display of colour which is hard to imagine when viewing the restored interiors of today. In the 15th century, wall paintings depicted scenes in the lives of saints and martyrs, a way of teaching a congregation unable to understand the Latin bible. After the 15th century, the primitive quality of the work, so full of feeling, disappeared under the hand of the accurate professional, a change that colours the whole of art history. Whitewashing, and the general destruction attendant upon the Suppression virtually destroyed all medieval wall painting. There are however notable attempts today to return, in part at least, to the original medieval colours. In restoration work, ribs and bosses, though not so much walls, have been brightly coloured to good effect.

WARMING-HOUSE

In the claustral buildings of a monastery, the so-called warming-house was the only room where fires were permitted. It is usually found under the dormitory.

WEATHER COCK

The weather-vane on the church spire indicates the changeableness of nature, and the cock symbolises the necessity for watchfulness by the spirit, so that the physical man may not be lead hither and thither by every wind that blows.

The changes in the winds are very much a part of the process of nature whereby the earth sacrifices itself in spring and summer to nourish the fruit and the flower, after which point the created forms are sacrificed back into the earth in autumn and winter. This continues the quest for perfection through recurrent cycles of growth. Thus the associations of development in the east and south winds (spring and summer) and of dying in the west and north winds (autumn and winter). (See 'cock' for its symbolism.)

Altar

Choir | Screen

West door

WEST END

'West' is from a Germanic stem *we*, 'down', which gives Latin *vesper*, 'evening' and Greek *hesperos*, 'evening'. The orientation of the church is discussed under East. The West is a symbol of materiality, extroversion towards the world, the waters of life as opposed to the spiritual sun of the East. It is connected with the general meaning of the word 'down', for man begins his life in the waters of the womb and then progresses to the realisation of the spirit from the experience the waters of life offer him. At the west end of the church are the stoup and font, both containing water, and the nave, the ship on the waters, whilst at the east end is the window allowing in the light of the rising sun. Thus the two poles in man, female and male, matter and spirit, are embodied in the form of the church. The journey between these poles is also symbolised in the great west door of the cathedral, which, when opened, aligns through the small gateway of the choir screen to the altar in the coveted sanctuary – the 'straight way and narrow gate'. (See 'East'.)

WHEEL-WINDOW

A name for the rose-window (q.v.) usually found on the west face of a cathedral and so called because of the spokes raying from the centre. The image of the wheel affirms the significance of the rose as a symbol of development: it is the wheel of life which moves men round inexorably, in order that the truth of the spirit (the East) may dawn in them. Generally, wheels in sculpture and painting in medieval times are such wheels of Fortune, pointing out the vicissitudes of human life.

WINDOW

Middle English *windowe*, from Old Norwegian *vindauga* (*vind*, 'wind' and *auga*, 'eye'). The original function of the glassless window was to keep out the elements and to let in light, as the two parts of the word indicate. Thus the thick windows of early churches were splayed so as to allow in as much light as possible. Because of this, in monastic settlements and Norman churches, religious images or decorations were perforce on the walls. It could be said that the inner light of the hermit had no need of the outer light of the world, and that conversely, as worship became more externalised, the external light penetrated the darkness until in the great cathedrals the interior was filled with the light from an expanse of multi-coloured windows. (See 'stained glass'.)

In the cathedrals, the transition from the simple openings of the late 12th century to the great spaces of the middle 16th century is reflected in the different styles of tracery (q.v.) which correspond broadly to different architectural periods. The following names are used to describe this tracery:

Lancet style with 'plate tracery' – circa 1190-1245
Geometric style with 'perfect tracery' – circa 1245-1315
Curvilinear style with 'flowing tracery' – circa 1315-1360
Rectilinear style with 'perpendicular tracery' – circa 1360-1550.

The last three of these are all forms of 'bar' tracery as opposed to plate tracery. (See 'tracery' for an explanation of this and for illustrations.)

In the first three there is considerable overlapping. Lancet, Geometric and Rectilinear do not exactly correspond with Early English and Decorated in architectural style. But the last, the 'perpendicular' tracery, is common to our parish churches and is accepted to span from the middle of the 14th to the 16th centuries. The most perfect tracery belongs to the geometric style with its simple circles and trefoils: here space and bar line are equally balanced.

WINE

See 'vine'.

WISDOM

From 'wis' and 'dom'. Middle English *wis*, from Old High German *wis*, 'wise', from an Aryan base 'to see': *dom* is an abbreviation of *dominus* 'Lord'. Thus, 'the wisdom or insight of the Lord'. In man, wisdom is the transcending of personal knowledge, the true end of religion, when the vision of man has become one with that of God.

WOOD-CARVING

Wood-carving in medieval churches did not assert its individual qualities until towards the end of the 14th century. The early work that has survived has no character and merely copies the stone mason's work in the tracery of windows. Decorations, with feeling for wood itself, developed in the 13th century with beautifully worked stalls, screens, bench ends, font-covers, pulpits and so on. Whereas the 13th and 14th centuries were the domain of the stone worker, the 15th was the domain of the wood-carver. At the same time, carpentry in the construction of roofs reached a peak in the 15th century with the arch brace, the beam and the hammer, whilst panelled roofs had beautifully carved bosses. Such excellence of wood-craft can be seen especially in the north of Britain, as at York, Beverley and Ripon, executed during the years 1490-1520, and equally in churches over the whole of Devon.

Carved screenwork and rood-lofts holding the cross all suffered irrevocably throughout the country at the time of the Suppression.

WYVERN or WIVERN

Middle English *wivers*, 'serpent', Latin *vipera*, 'viper'. A fabulous animal used heraldically, usually shown with wings, head and tail of a scorpion, and two legs.

Y

YEW

Old English *ēow*, from Old High German *iwa*, 'yew'. The Latin for yew, *taxus*, is related to Greek *toxon*, 'bow', because the yew was the finest wood for bow-making, and to *toxicon*, 'poison', because the arrows of the primitive Greeks were tipped with poison.

The yew is traditionally the tree of death, and is found growing in churchyards – yet the sound of the word and nature of the tree itself (the affirmative 'y' and the length of life of the tree) suggest the opposite. It is an evergreen and lives to a longer age than the oak, some in Britain reputedly being between two and three thousand years old. Also, when polished, the wood has a capacity for resisting natural processes of decay. Thus in European legend, though it is the tree of death, there is also the aspect of immortality. As in all symbols, opposite faces are seen together, and to the Druids the yews near their temples denoted eternal life out of physical death.

Z

ZIG-ZAG

A type of moulding of zig-zag pattern used particularly in Norman architecture. (See 'chevron'.)